T0087763

Living as a Bird

Living as a Bird

Vinciane Despret

Translated by Helen Morrison

polity

Originally published in French as *Habiter en oiseau* © Actes Sud, France, 2019

This English edition © Polity Press, 2022

Epigraph from *Nous sommes à la lisière* by Caroline Lamarche © Gallimard 2019. Reprinted with kind permission of Gallimard.

Polity Press
65 Bridge Street
Cambridge CB2 1UR, UK

Polity Press
101 Station Landing
Suite 300
Medford, MA 02155, USA

All rights reserved. Except for the quotation of short passages for the purpose of criticism and review, no part of this publication may be reproduced, stored in a retrieval system or transmitted, in any form or by any means, electronic, mechanical, photocopying, recording or otherwise, without the prior permission of the publisher.

ISBN-13: 978-1-5095-4726-5
ISBN-13: 978-1-5095-4727-2 (paperback)

A catalogue record for this book is available from the British Library.

Library of Congress Cataloging-in-Publication Data

Names: Despret, Vinciane, author. | Morrison, Helen (Langauge translator), translator.
Title: Living as a bird / Vinciane Despret ; translated by Helen Morrison.
Other titles: Habiter en oiseau. English
Description: Cambridge ; Medford, MA : Polity Press, [2021] | "Originally published in French as Habiter en oiseau © Actes Sud, France, 2019." | Includes bibliographical references.
Identifiers: LCCN 2021016407 (print) | LCCN 2021016408 (ebook) | ISBN 9781509547265 (hardback) | ISBN 9781509547272 (paperback) | ISBN 9781509547289 (epub)
Subjects: LCSH: Birds--Territoriality. | Birds--Behavior. | Birds--Research. | Territoriality (Zoology)--Philosophy.
Classification: LCC QL678 .D4713 2021 (print) | LCC QL678 (ebook) | DDC 598--dc23
LC record available at https://lccn.loc.gov/2021016407
LC ebook record available at https://lccn.loc.gov/2021016408

Typeset in 11 on 14 pt Fournier and 10.25 on 14 pt Brandon Grotesque
by Cheshire Typesetting Ltd, Cuddington, Cheshire
Printed and bound in Great Britain by TJ Books Ltd, Padstow, Cornwall

The publisher has used its best endeavours to ensure that the URLs for external websites referred to in this book are correct and active at the time of going to press. However, the publisher has no responsibility for the websites and can make no guarantee that a site will remain live or that the content is or will remain appropriate.

Every effort has been made to trace all copyright holders, but if any have been overlooked the publisher will be pleased to include any necessary credits in any subsequent reprint or edition.

For further information on Polity, visit our website:
politybooks.com

For Donna Haraway, Bruno Latour and Isabelle Stengers

Contents

Contents

POSTSCRIPTS

Acknowledgements

My thanks to:

Alexandra Elbakyan, whose tireless work in sharing and making available countless scientific articles made this research possible.

Stéphane Durand, who gave me the idea for this book, encouraged, supported, commented on and read my work with extraordinary generosity.

Baptiste Morizot, who gave the book its title, its momentum and many more invaluable things besides.

Marcos Matteos Dias for the melodic breathing.

Thibault De Meyer for everything he shares with me, for his notes which so pertinently understand and help others understand what matters, for his emails and his generous rereading.

Maud Hagelstein, not only for reading the manuscript with such extraordinary attention but especially for her enthusiasm and support, so precious in that perilous moment when you find yourself wondering if you should even have written it.

Isabelle Stengers, from the very beginning to the very last lines.

All the people who agreed to discuss my research and who often made me see things in an unexpected light: Serge Gutwirth and his team of researchers on '*commonings*'; my colleagues from the research centre 'Matérialités de la politique' at Liège University – in particular Florence Caeymaex, Édouard Delruelle, Jérôme Flas, Antoine

Acknowledgements

Janvier and Ferhat Taylan; Sophie Houdart, Marc Boissenade, Élisabeth Claverie, Patricia Falguières, Élisabeth Lebovici from the Call it Anything collective; Tomas Saraceno, Ally Bisshop and Filipa Ramos.

Pauline Bastin and her decoys, Laurent Jacob, who reminded me about the disappearance of birds, for their welcome and their company.

Laurence Bouquiaux and Julien Pieron, for their interest and their friendship.

Roger Delcommune, Christophe and Céline Caron, Samuel Lemaire and Cindy Colette, and Lola Delœuvre who, in one way or another, made my life, and Alba's, so very much more comfortable while I was working.

My family, Jean Marie Lemaire, Jules-Vincent, Sarah and Elioth Buono-Lemaire, Samuel and Cindy once again, who supported me and reminded me that life is about more than just writing.

And Alba, for her infinite patience.

FIRST CHORD

Counterpoint

There are more things between heaven and earth (the realm of birds) than our philosophy can easily explain.

Étienne Souriau[1]

It all began with a blackbird. My bedroom window had remained open for the first time for many months, a symbol of victory over the winter. The blackbird's song woke me at dawn. He was singing with all his heart, with all his strength, with all his blackbird talent. From a little further away, probably from a nearby chimney, another bird replied. I could not get back to sleep. This blackbird was singing, as the philosopher Étienne Souriau would say, with all *the enthusiasm* of his body, as animals do when they are utterly absorbed in their play and in the simulation of whatever it is they are acting out.[2] Yet it was not this enthusiasm that kept me awake, nor what an ill-humoured biologist might have called a noisy demonstration of evolutionary success. It was the sustained determination of this blackbird to vary each series of notes. From the second or third call, I was spellbound by what was transforming into an audiophonic novel, each episode of which I greeted with an unspoken 'and what next?' Each sequence differed from the preceding one; each was reinvented as a new and original counterpoint.

From that day on, my window remained open every night. With each successive sleepless episode like the one I experienced that first

3

morning, I rediscovered the same surprise, the same sense of anticipation which prevented me from going back to sleep (or even wishing
to do so). The bird sang. But never before had song seemed so close
to speech. These were phrases. Recognizable as such. They caught my
ear in exactly the same way as words themselves would do. And yet,
in that sustained effort imposed by the urge to avoid repetition, never
had song seemed further removed from language. This was speech, but
taut with beauty and where every single word mattered. The silence
held its breath and I felt it tremble in tune with the song. I had the
most clear and intense feeling that, at that moment, the fate of the
entire world, or perhaps the existence of beauty itself, rested on the
shoulders of this blackbird.

Étienne Souriau referred to the enthusiasm of the body. The composer Bernard Fort told me that certain ornithologists use the word
'exaltation' with reference to skylarks.[3] For this blackbird, the word
'importance' imposed itself above all else. Something mattered, more
than anything else, and nothing else mattered except the act of singing. And whatever it was that mattered was invented in a blackbird's
song, suffusing it completely, transporting it, carrying it onwards, to
others, to the other blackbird nearby, to my body straining to hear it,
to the furthest limits to which its strength could convey it. Perhaps
that feeling I had of a total silence, clearly impossible given the urban
environment beyond my window, was evidence that this sense of
importance had seized me so powerfully that everything outside that
song had ceased to exist. The song had brought me silence. The sense
of importance had imposed itself on me.

Perhaps also the song affected me so powerfully because I had
recently read *The Companion Species Manifesto* by Donna Haraway.[4]
In this extremely beautiful book, the philosopher describes the relationship that she has forged with her dog, Cayenne. She explains how

this relationship has had a profound effect on the way she relates to other beings, or, more precisely, to 'relations of significant otherness', how it has taught her to become more aware of the world around her, more closely attuned to it, more curious, and how she hopes that the experiences she has shared with Cayenne will stimulate an appetite for new forms of commitment with other beings who will one day matter in the same way. What Haraway's book *does*, and I was struck by this in the context of my own experience, is to stimulate, encourage and bring into existence, to render attractive, other modes of attention.[5] And to focus attention on these forms of attentiveness. It is a matter not of becoming more sensitive (a rather too convenient hotchpotch of a notion which could just as easily lead to allergies) but of learning *how* to pay attention and becoming capable of doing so. *Paying attention* here with an added sense of being attuned, of 'giving your attention' to other beings and at the same time acknowledging the way other beings are themselves attentive. It is another way of acknowledging importance.

The ethnologist Daniel Fabre would often describe his profession as one which focused attention on whatever prevented people from sleeping. The anthropologist Eduardo Viveiros de Castro came up with a very similar definition of anthropology, describing it as the study of variations of importance. He writes moreover that, 'if there is something that *de jure* belongs to anthropology, it is not the task of explaining the world of the other but that of multiplying our world.'[6] I believe that many of the ethologists who observe and study animals, following in the footsteps of the naturalists who preceded them and who took this task so much to heart, invite us to follow a similar path: that of becoming aware of, of multiplying '*modes of existence*' – in other words, 'ways of experiencing, of feeling, of making sense, and of granting importance to things'.[7] When the ethologist Marc Bekoff says that each animal is a way of knowing the world, he is saying the same thing. Scientists cannot, of course, dispense with explanations altogether, but explaining can take many very diverse forms. It can, for example, be a way of reconfiguring complicated stories as the vagaries of life which stubbornly insists on trying out every possible variation, or it can mean trying to seek answers for puzzling problems, the solutions to which have already been invented by this or that animal, but it can also reflect a determination to find a general all-purpose theory to which everything would conform. Put another way, there are explanations which end up multiplying worlds and celebrating the emergence of an infinite number of modes of existence and others which seek to impose order, bringing them back to a few basic principles.

The blackbird had begun to sing. Something mattered to him, and at that moment nothing else existed except the overriding obligation to allow something to be heard. Was he hailing the end of the winter? Was he singing about the sheer joy of existing, the sense of feeling himself alive once again? Was he offering up praise to the cosmos? Scientists would probably steer clear of such language. But they could nevertheless assert that all the cosmic forces of an emerging spring had converged to provide the blackbird with the preliminary conditions for his metamorphosis.[8] For this is indeed a metamorphosis. This blackbird, who had probably lived through a relatively peaceful winter, albeit a challenging one, punctuated from time to time by a few unconvincing moments of indignation towards his fellow creatures, intent on maintaining a low profile and living a quiet life, is now singing his heart out, perched on the highest and most visible spot he could find. And everything that the blackbird had experienced and felt over the last few months, everything which had, until that moment, given meaning to things and to other creatures, now becomes part of a new importance, one which is urgent and insistent and which will totally modify his manner of being. He has become territorial.

Territories

Unicum arbustum haud alit
Duos erithacos

> (A single tree cannot shelter two robins)
> Proverb by Zenodotus of Ephesus
> (Greek philosopher, third century BC)

Scientists have found themselves genuinely intrigued by this process of metamorphosis. And not just intrigued, but moved at the same time. How can these birds, some of whom have been observed quietly living together through the winter, flying in unison, seeking food together, sometimes squabbling over apparently trivial matters, somehow, at a given moment, adopt a completely different attitude? From that point on, they isolate themselves from other birds, select a particular place and confine themselves to it, singing ceaselessly from one of their chosen promontories. Seemingly no longer able to tolerate the presence of their fellow creatures, they furiously devote all their energy to a frenzy of threats and attacks if any of these dares to cross a line, invisible to our eyes, but which appears to represent a remarkably well-defined border. The strangeness of their behaviour is astonishing enough, but even more striking is the aggressivity, the utter determination and pugnacity of their reactions towards others and, above all, what will later be referred to as the incredible 'profusion' of songs and poses – colours, dances, flights, movements of the most extravagant nature, all of them spectacular, all of them elements of a veritable spectacle. And the equally astonishing repetition of the routines involved in the process of setting up a territory. In 1920, Henry Eliot Howard described how a male reed bunting, observed from his home in the English countryside of Worcestershire, set about establishing his territory. The bird chose a marshy area planted with small alders and willows. Any of these trees would have provided a suitable perch from which to survey the surrounding area, but the bunting chose one in particular, which would in a sense become the most important spot in the chosen area, the bird's 'headquarters', as Howard would call them. This would be the base from which he would signal his presence by his singing, monitor the movements of his neighbours and go off in search of food. Howard observed a specific routine taking shape around what would become the centre of the bird's territory: the bird would leave the tree, go and perch in a nearby shrub, then on a bulrush a little further away, before returning once more to the tree. These journeys would be repeated in all directions with remarkable regularity. Their endless repetition mapped out the territory and gradually established its limits.

Other descriptions are possible. These would quickly follow, since Howard had clearly opened the floodgates to a whole stream of research in this area and was widely acknowledged by all the scientists working in this field as its genuine founder. His book *Territory in Bird Life*, published in 1920, not only provides meticulously detailed descriptions but also sets out a coherent theory which provides the explanation for these observations. According to Howard, the birds are engaged in securing a territory which will enable them to mate, build a nest, protect their young and find enough food to provide for their brood.

I should point out, first of all, that Howard was not a professional scientist but, rather, a naturalist who was passionate about observing birds, an activity to which he devoted the first hours of each day, before going to work. But scientists would quickly follow in his footsteps, acknowledging him as the true pioneer of this new field of research. Territory, as Howard understood it, could now be regarded as a valid scientific subject and could be explained in terms of the 'functions' it sustained in relation to the survival of the species. Moreover, in order to signal the arrival of this subject in the scientific domain, ornithologists would refer to a 'pre-territorial' period, indicating any theoretical speculations which preceded Howard. Secondly, it should also be pointed out that Howard was not in fact the first person to have associated territorial behaviour with the functions it could sustain and with the demands of reproduction. Two other writers had done so before him, notably Bernard Altum, the German zoologist who, in 1868, in a book which would not however be translated until considerably later, had developed a detailed theory of territory, and another amateur, Charles Moffat, a journalist with a passion for natural history, whose writings, published in 1903 in the relatively obscure *Irish Naturalist's Journal*, would escape the notice of scientists. If Howard is acknowledged as the true pioneer of research in this area, it is first of all because he was the first writer, among those *read* by English and American ornithologists, to propose a detailed and coherent theory in a domain hitherto dominated by a great many speculative hypotheses.[1] In addition, Howard was responsible for the growing popularity of a new method focusing on the *life stories* of individual birds. This is significant in that it was a matter not just of telling the story of birds but of becoming familiar with their 'lives'. We should not forget that, until then, many ornithologists and amateurs studied birds largely by killing them or by taking their eggs to form collections or to draw up categories.

What scientists refer to as the 'pre-territorial period' in relation to the theory of territory therefore indicates the fact that any observations tended to be relatively fragmentary in nature and lacked any real theoretical structure. The proverb from Zenodotus cited as an epigraph to this chapter, for example, would be revived at a later stage in connection with the theory that robins like solitude. Before Zenodotus, Aristotle had observed, in his *Historia animalium*, that animals, and, more specifically, eagles, defend the area which constitutes their feeding ground. He also observed the fact that, in certain areas, where food was in short supply, only one pair of ravens would be found.

For others, territory would first of all be associated with rivalry between males over females. The defended area would either enable the male to ensure exclusive access to any female who settled there, and would therefore amount to a problem of jealousy, or it would provide him with a 'stage' on which to sing and perform displays in order to attract a potential partner. This would be one of Moffat's theories. In such a case, territory counts not as a space but as a behavioural whole.

Not surprisingly, the hypothesis of the robin's love of solitude failed to gain a place in any scientific writings. The theory arguing that a territory enables a bird to guarantee exclusive access to the resources necessary to its survival would, by contrast, long be considered a pertinent one and would gain favour with a great many ornithologists. The argument that territory is associated with a problem of competition around females would, however, dominate the preterritorial scene for a considerable time (and was notably favoured by Darwin). Controversial as it was, it would not be completely abandoned and would recur frequently, in one form or another, in scientific writings – no doubt encouraged by the attraction certain scientists have for the high drama often involved in competition and in others (sometimes involving the same people) because of a reluctance to abandon the notion that females are simply resources for males. Howard, however, vigorously challenged this theory of competition around females because it failed to fit certain of his observations. He wrote moreover that it held only for as long as it was believed that such confrontations exclusively involved males. In fact, as he pointed out, in certain species females fought with other females, couples with couples, or even sometimes a couple of birds might attack a solitary male or female. And what explanation might be given for the fact that, in species which travel to breeding sites, the males sometimes arrive considerably in advance of the females and immediately engage in conflict? Territorial behaviour nevertheless remains a predominantly male affair. As Howard points out, if the females behaved in the same way and isolated themselves, birds would never succeed in getting together!

The notion that birds could establish living spaces and would then protect their exclusive right to such zones is not a new one and had already been observed by Aristotle, Zenodotus and some later writers. However, the term 'territory' was not mentioned and would appear for the first time with reference to birds only in the course of the seventeenth century. In her book on this subject, published in 1941, Margaret Morse Nice, an American ornithologist, indicates that the first reference to territory occurs in a book by John Ray (1627–1705) entitled *The Ornithology of Francis Willughby* and published in 1678. As the title suggests, Ray's book focuses on the work carried out by his friend Francis Willughby (1635–1672). With reference to the common nightingale, Ray cites another writer, Giovanni Pietro Olina, who published a treatise on ornithology entitled *Uccelliera, ovvero, Discorso della natura, e proprietà di diversi uccelli* in Rome in 1622. This treatise turns out to be a book on the various ways of catching and looking after birds in order to set up aviaries: 'It is proper to this Bird at his first coming (saith Olina) to occupy or seize upon one place as its Freehold, into which it will not admit any other Nightingale but its mate.' Ray also mentions the fact, again according to Olina, that the nightingale 'has a peculiarity that it cannot abide a companion in the place where it lives and will attack with all its strength any who dispute this claim.'[2] But according to ornithologists Tim Birkhead and Sophie Van Balen,[3] another writer, Antonio Valli da Todi, in fact preceded Olina in 1601 with a book on birdsong, and it is highly likely, given how similar the observations are in both books, that the latter may have copied his predecessor. He describes, for example, how the nightingale 'chooses a freehold, in which it will admit no other nightingale but its female, and if other nightingales try to enter that place, it starts singing in the centre of this site.' Valli da Todi would estimate the size of this territory by observing that its extent corresponded to a long stone's throw. It should be noted incidentally that Valli da Todi himself derived much of his information from a work by Manzini, published in 1575. This latter does not, however, discuss the issue of territory.

We could of course allow ourselves to reflect on a coincidence here in that the term 'territory', with its very strong connotation of 'the taking over of an exclusive area or property', first appears in ornithological literature in the seventeenth century – in other words, at the very moment when, according to Philippe Descola and a great many legal historians, the Moderns reduced the use of land to a single concept, that of appropriation.[4] Descola emphasizes that this conception is now so widely accepted that it would be very difficult to abandon it. In short, this notion first took shape under the influence of Grotius and the concept of natural law,[5] although it is in fact rooted in sixteenth-century theology. It redefines the right of ownership as an individual right and is based in part on the idea of a contract which redefines humans as individuals and not as social beings (the 'ownership' of Roman law came about as the result of a process of sharing and not of an individual act, a sharing sanctioned by the law, the customs and the courts). In addition, it drew both on new techniques for evaluating land, which meant that any land would be delineated and its possession assured, and on a philosophical theory of the subject, that of possessive individualism, which reconfigures political society as a mechanism for the protection of individual property. We are all too aware of the dramatic consequences of this new conception of ownership, of those it favoured and of those whose lives were destroyed as a result. We are familiar with the history of enclosure, the expulsion of peasant communities from land over which they had previously exercised commoners' rights and the ban which prevented them from taking from the forests the resources essential to their survival. With this new conception of ownership came the eradication of what is generally referred to today as the 'commons' and which represented land given over to the collective, coordinated and self-organized use of shared resources, such as irrigation ditches, common grazing grounds and forests[6] . . . In England, writes Karl Polanyi, 'in 1600, half of the kingdom's arable land was still in communal use. By 1750, that figure had fallen to only a quarter and amounted to almost none at all in 1840.'[7] Of the many different ways of inhabiting and sharing the land which had been invented and cultivated over the course of centuries, all that would remain would be the right of ownership, admittedly sometimes limited, but always defined as an exclusive right to use, and indeed abuse.

Returning to birds, to nightingales and to robins, I am not however entirely convinced that very much can be learned from this historical coincidence. That would be going rather too fast. It would mean, for example, neglecting the fact that the term 'territory' was not used in a random way with reference to animals but only in the description of the methods used to confine birds within aviaries, methods involving appropriation admittedly, and which involved the uses of cages and confinement but also methods intended to deterritorialize birds in order to have them live 'with us', in what constitutes 'our' territories. If I am to use this coincidence as a starting point from which to explore the story of territory, should I not also point out that the aviary originates from the desire to protect harvests from birds? And, at the same time, should I not emphasize that, as a result, it was linked to the art of hunting and falconry, an art that required cunning and an intimate knowledge of the habits of the various birds? Thus, for example, in the fourteenth century, pheasants were hunted with a mirror as a consequence of the observation that 'a male cannot abide the presence of another' and would immediately provoke a confrontation. A mirror would be hung from a string and the pheasant, convinced that what it was seeing in its reflection was one of its own kind, would attack the mirror, crashing into it and triggering the release of a cage which would then fall down and act as a trap. But if I am indeed to tell this story, I should also point out that it was precisely in the seventeenth century that aviaries ceased to be associated with falconry and that, instead, birds would be captured on a large scale no longer purely with the intention of killing them but for the pleasure of living alongside them and hearing their songs.[8] This unprecedented enthusiasm for aviaries tended to focus on songbirds in particular – that is to say, in the vast majority of cases, territorial birds. This led to a spate of treatises describing their habits, their uses, the different ways of catching them and of keeping them alive. And I would no doubt need a great many more stories in order to consolidate this coincidence, to come up with other ways of linking these two events, to breathe life into a world I know little about but which – particularly in the context of this investigation – I have inherited. But if I am unable to do this, and if I must leave this coincidence as an open question, I can still be grateful for the fact that this process encourages me to be vigilant: 'territory' is by no means an innocent term, and I must not allow myself to lose sight of the violent forms of appropriation and of the destruction which has been associated with some of its current manifestations. It is a term which could bring in its wake certain habits of thinking as impoverished as the multiple uses which had characterized the reality of inhabiting and sharing the earth from the seventeenth century onwards.

Caution is therefore required. And curiosity. I have of course come across some examples of terms which are at the very least ambiguous, such as the fact that a male 'claims' a space, that he establishes 'possession' or that hummingbirds defend a 'private hunting ground'. The fact that, in the context of territorial behaviour, aggressivity should be so prevalent and apparently so specific has also attracted a certain type of attention, particularly since observers, associating it with the usual patterns of competition, have tended to interpret it quite literally, emphasizing its aversive effect. The words used by some ornithologists to describe specific behaviours speak volumes: conflicts, combats, challenges, disputes, attacks, chases, patrols, territorial defence, headquarters (frequently used in reference to the central point of the territory from which the bird sings), war paint (to describe the colours of territorial birds) . . . But, at a very early stage, certain ornithologists challenged these terminological practices, not because they anthropomorphize birds but because they tend to focus attention on competitive and aggressive behaviour associated with territorialization, to the detriment of other dimensions which seemed to them of crucial importance.

That apart, as I was to discover in the course of my investigation, few ornithologists favour an approach based on 'ownership'. The majority would prefer the definition proposed in 1939 by the American zoologist Gladwyn Kingsley Noble, 'Territory is any defended area.' This at least had the merit of being a relatively simple one, capable of describing almost all territorial situations. Depending on the various theories, a variety of functions would also be identified: a site can be defended in order to ensure subsistence, to protect birds from interference during the reproductive period, to provide a 'stage' for 'promotion' (a term encompassing all forms of exhibition, displays and songs), to ensure exclusive rights over a female or guarantee the stability of the same meeting place from one year to another, along with various other functions which will be examined in chapter 2. Very quickly, ornithologists realized that there was no *one* single way of establishing a territory but instead multiple forms of territorialization. This definition of an 'actively defended area' would be subject to a great many nuances as more discoveries on the subject came to light and as the multiplicity of different ways of becoming territorial were revealed. The boundaries would turn out to be far more flexible, negotiable and porous than early observations might have indicated, and, surprisingly perhaps, certain researchers would reach the conclusion that, for many birds, territories had other functions beyond simply that of protection against intrusion and ensuring exclusive use of a site. All of that will be examined in what follows.

Territory will therefore take on other meanings which extend well beyond the notion that it is simply a matter of property. Certain ornithologists were moreover at pains to point out that, when it comes to territory, what is said with reference to birds does not necessarily have the same meaning as humans would give to the term. Howard, for example, would emphasize that territory is above all a process, or rather, as he explains, part of a process involved in the reproduction cycle: 'Regarded thus, we avoid the risk of conceiving of the act of securing a territory as a detached event in the life of a bird, and avoid, I hope, the risk of a conception based upon the meaning of the word when used to describe human as opposed to animal procedures.'[9] A few pages further on, he would add that what he calls a disposition to secure a territory amounts to a disposition to remain in a particular place at a particular moment. And even the father of ethology, Konrad Lorenz, whose book *On Aggression* is certainly by no means exempt from questionable and insufficiently problematized analogies, was keen to distinguish between territory and property, pointing out that territory 'must not be imagined as a property determined by geographical confines.'[10] Territory, he adds, can also, in certain circumstances and for certain animals, be linked as much to time as it is to space. Thus, for example, cats establish what he calls 'a definite timetable': a given space is not divided but instead shared at different times. The cats leave scent marks at regular intervals. If a cat encounters one of these marks, it can assess whether it is fresh or a few hours old. In the first case the cat chooses a different route and in the second it continues calmly on its way. These marks, according to Lorenz, 'act like railway signals whose aim is to prevent collision between two trains'.

Yet the cautious approach taken by Lorenz vis-à-vis possible misunderstandings (a caution which is very much relative since, on the same page, we will nonetheless be confronted with the notion of territory as a 'headquarters') is not quite as widely shared as might be suggested by what has so far been described. I have been referring to ornithologists, but they are not alone in taking an interest in animal territories. And that, as we say in colloquial terms, is where things take a turn for the worse.[11]

So, for example, in the historical inventory drawn up by the ornithologist Margaret Nice, I find a quotation from Walter Heape, who writes, in a book on emigration, immigration and nomadism published at the end of the 1920s, that

> territorial rights are established rights among the majority of species of animals. There can be no doubt that the desire for acquisition of a definite territorial area, the determination to hold it by fighting if necessary, and the recognition of individual as well as of tribal territorial rights by others are dominant in all animals. In fact, it may be held that the recognition of territorial rights, one of the most significant attributes of civilisation, was not evolved by man, but has been an inherent factor in the life history of all animals.[12]

Need I point out that Heape is an embryologist and not an ornithologist? Should I also take into consideration information I discovered in probing a little deeper, notably the fact that he became famous for having successfully carried out, in 1890, the first transfer of embryos from an angora rabbit into the uterus of a female domestic rabbit (the Belgian hare), inseminated three hours earlier by a male of its own species? Does that have any bearing here? Could it be that the success of this transfer between two different types of creature (the two angora rabbits and the four little Belgian hares born as a result of the experiment are testimony to the success of the operation) might perhaps have encouraged Heape, like a form of authorization awarded to himself, to indulge in other types of transfer, without considering that these might involve risks of an entirely different nature, requiring very different precautions? In advancing such a hypothesis, I am, of course, guilty of exaggeration and, in a sense, am deliberately crossing boundaries myself, without due precaution, and in ways which may not always be in the best of taste. For it is not only a matter of style which is at stake in such analogies and comparisons, a matter of political or epistemological style, it is also a matter of taste. Isabelle Stengers proposes restoring Kant's '*sapere aude*', 'dare to know', to its original meaning, attributed to it by the Roman poet Horace: 'Dare to taste.' Learning to know something, she says, means learning to discriminate, learning to recognize what matters, learning how differences count, and learning all of that in the context of the encounter with all its attendant risks and consequences. In other words, it means connecting with the inherent plurality of what matters for these *particular beings*, the ones we are trying to get to know, and of what matters because of them. It is an art of consequences.[13]

It is precisely for this reason that I was filled with dismay on reading Michel Serres' book *Malfeasance*.[14] A sensation all the more acute because, until then, his efforts to 'deterritorialize' issues and concepts, to take them out of their fields of study and remove them from the temporalities in which they had been associated, represented a creative task which was at once daring and imaginative, teeming with connections, with translations, and with potentially rich and inventive relationships. Thus, in *The Natural Contract*,[15] when he asks the question 'What language do the things of the world speak, that we might come to an understanding with them, contractually?', we are aware of the presence of an authentic network of analogies, which I would describe as generative, of analogies which enrich the terms of comparison, analogies which, through a series of interconnections, make us aware of qualities hitherto unperceived, and which are capable of reactivating an exchange of the forces of action, or agencies, between objects and living creatures. So is it with the earth, which, Serres tells us, speaks in terms of forces, of bonds and of interactions. In a later book, *Darwin, Bonaparte et le Samaritain: une philosophie de l'histoire*, Serres returns to this idea again, this time focusing more precisely on writing. Reading, he says, is not limited only to the codes of writing such as we normally understand it, and this is exemplified by good hunters, accustomed to reading, in the tracks left by wild boars, their age, gender, weight, size and a thousand other details: 'The good hunter reads, having learned how to read. What does he decipher? A coded footprint. Yet this definition could equally well be applied to historic human writing itself.'[16] Because, Serres goes on to say, writing is the *line* traced by all beings, living or non-living, all of whom write 'on things and between them, the things of the world one on top of the other'. The ocean writes on the rocky cliff, bacteria write on our bodies, everything – fossils, erosions, strata, the glow of galaxies, the crystallization of volcanic rocks – is *there* to be read. We could read before we could write, and this possibility opens writing to a great many other registers, like 'an ensemble of traces which encode a meaning'. 'If history begins with writing, then all the sciences enter, along with the world, a new history, one which does not forget.' Of course, these are daring juxtapositions on the part of Serres, interpretations which link what seemed destined to remain unlinked – if only because human exceptionalism keeps a careful watch over these separations of register. And this is precisely what Serres is interested in, this task of abandoning the sordid habit of placing the human at the centre of the world and of its stories, and instead opening history to myriads of beings which matter and without which we would not be here.

Malfeasance takes a very different subject, as is clear from the book's subtitle: *Appropriation through Pollution*? From the very first pages, Serres turns his attention to territories: 'Tigers piss on the edge of their lair. And so do lions and dogs. Like those carnivorous mammals, many animals, our cousins, *mark* their territory with their harsh, stinking urine or with their howling, while others such as finches and nightingales use sweet songs.'[17] Such practices, according to Serres, are the ways in which the living inhabit a specific space, establish it and recognize it. These places are defined and protected by male excrement. All of them constitute different ways of appropriating, whether by men or by animals: 'Whoever spits in the soup keeps it; no one will touch the salad or the cheese polluted in this way. To make something its own, the body knows how to leave some personal stain: sweat on a garment, saliva or feet put into a dish, waste in space, aroma, perfume, or excrement, all of them rather hard things . . .'[18] Serres then observes that the verb 'to have', expressing possession, has the same origin in Latin as 'to inhabit'. 'From the mists of time', he writes, 'our languages echo the profound relationship between the nest and appropriation, between the living space and possession: I inhabit, therefore I have.'[19] For Serres, the act of appropriating stems from 'an animal origin that is ethological, bodily, psychological, organic, vital . . . .' not from a convention or from some positive right: 'I sense there', he writes, 'a collection of urine, blood, excretions, rotting corpses.'[20] I have indicated already that, in this context, Serres is no longer concerned with a fight against anthropocentrism and against this strange historical amnesia to anything which is not human. His mission in this case is to mount an attack on all forms of appropriation through pollution, whether air pollution, the invasion of visual or sound space to which we are submitted in the form of advertising, cars, machines . . . all of them just as filthy and polluting as the excrements used to signal appropriation. 'You obtain and keep what is properly yours through dirt,' he writes, or, even more explicitly, 'The spit spoils the soup, the logo the object, the signature the page: *property, propriety, or cleanliness*. The same word tells of the same struggle; in French, it has the same origin and the same meaning. Property *is marked*, just as the footstep leaves its imprint.'[21]

But this is not the reason for my severity towards him – quite the contrary in fact. That Serres should want to make us aware of, and outraged by, all the various market-driven operations of expropriation and appropriation is not the issue here, and I very much share his opinion on that subject. However, the fact that, for him, garbage and marks, as soiling gestures, are of animal origin seems to me all the more seriously problematic in that the gesture of appropriation is, in his view, synonymous with that of disappropriation and exclusion.[22] The equation is too hasty. For this connection can be made only at the cost of a double simplification, a double negligence. Firstly, because it means forgetting that, for a tiger, a dog or a nightingale, territory does not equate to this or, indeed, to any one 'single' thing which could claim to unify a certain combination of types of behaviour. And, secondly, because this definition of ownership as a process of monopolizing and taking over seems to me to define living in a territory in too facile and simplistic a manner. By advocating a form of naturality in terms of territorial behaviour as an argument to denounce the right assumed by some people to pollute the air, the acoustic environment, shared things and space, Serres, without pause for question, associates the territorial behaviour of animals with a regime of possession and ownership and, as a result, assimilates it to a form of natural rights. In short, he attributes a modern and unchallenged conception of ownership to animals, turning the latter into petty little bourgeois property owners preoccupied with claiming exclusive ownership.

For me, it is not about wanting to defend the violated dignity of these animals caught up in a project which sets out to defend a damaged earth or polluted existences. But if we are indeed to reflect on the reappropriation of the earth, I believe that it is important to pay attention to the different ways of inhabiting it and to those who inhabit it alongside us. With this oversimplified ethology we are off to a very bad start.

It should be pointed out first of all that it is highly questionable to associate animal markings with dirtiness and to regard the latter as somehow the opposite of cleanliness. It is *us*, or most of us, who see excrement as dirty, but for many animals things are much more complicated. Anyone who has watched their dog wallowing enthusiastically in a decaying carcase or rolling in animal droppings will immediately understand that, as far as smells are concerned, we inhabit completely different universes. Secondly, putting mammals and birds in the same category is not really a good idea. True, marking and singing appear to share a common function in that both are done in order to signal presence. But mammals and birds have very different problems to resolve when it comes to announcing their presence and any similarities should be approached with considerable caution. It makes little sense to refer simply to 'animals'. If certain birds – though this is more unusual – can indeed mark their presence by their droppings, they generally tend to favour the use of song and of what might be called intense demonstrations of their physical presence. Mammals, for the most part, have opted simply to suggest their presence. For most birds, territory is a site for display and spectacle. It is the place which enables the bird to be both seen and heard. Indeed, it would be perfectly reasonable to wonder if in certain cases (in the case of leks, or mating grounds, this is indisputably how things stand) it is not so much in order to defend their territory that birds sing and perform their various displays as that the territory provides them with a stage for those songs and displays. Some ornithologists have indeed suggested this to be the case.

Clearly many mammals have a very different ambition and therefore correspond closely to Jean-Christophe Bailly's proposed definition of territory as a place where it is possible to hide, or, more precisely, a place where animals know where to hide.[23] Songs and tracks or traces therefore already have only superficial similarities. It could be said that mammals are experts in the use of the metaphor *in absentia* – the tracks and traces *suggest* presence so that animals make their presence felt in their absence. For birds, on the other hand, having chosen the more literal choice of 'Here I am', everything is pretext for being seen and heard. One writer uses the term 'broadcasting' in reference to this process, a term which suggests dissemination, and this is clearly the case here, but one which also refers to advertising or promotion via the media (radio or television).[24] If the term 'broadcasting' can be applied to both birds and mammals, it would nevertheless be used somewhat differently in each case. In the case of birds, the focus would be very much on the notion of 'promotion', of advertising, whereas for mammals who mark their territory, it would refer to the fact that not only are the transmitter and the message in different locations, but that the transmitter is able to leave multiple indications of presence by making sure every trace or mark left behind continues to broadcast its presence. The deferred power of ubiquity through messages.

Mammals need to resolve a problem which is much less difficult for birds, notably that of being present everywhere. Birds have the advantage of a much greater mobility and are capable of flying over their territory rapidly from one point to another, which is not the case for mammals, particularly since the latter seek to remain hidden.

The problem of movement in space – the ability, or inability, to be everywhere at once – and that of needing to be seen or to remain hidden have been resolved in each case through a different relationship between presence and time. Birds, with their songs and displays, are in a regime of physical presence, whereas mammals, with their marking activities, have adopted a regime of historical presence. The tracks left behind by a mammal continue to be effective over a relatively long time (in relation to its actual presence at the site), with the animal seemingly present everywhere at the same time even though in fact any actual presence occurred some while previously. Droppings might in this context be seen as a kind of decoy, in that they create the effect of a presence in absence. But it is a decoy that fails to deceive anybody (though that does not affect its efficacy), since each message conveys an element of 'watch out!', or 'be careful!' And the message finds its mark. The traces or tracks left by the animal are therefore part of this process referred to as 'stigmergy', or 'non-local rules of interaction' through which the behaviour of certain animals can – whether in space or in time – affect the behaviours of others at a distance – just as ants leave behind them the pheromones which will alter the route of those following on behind. It is a form of presence which creates certain modes of attention. Moreover, it is rather sad that Serres, who so appositely succeeded in using the argument of writing in its broadest sense to portray the traces and tracks left by animals as the astonishingly sophisticated mechanisms of writing, capable of conveying a wide range of qualities and messages, should fail to consider, or rather deliberately choose to forget, that the hunter is not the only one to read tracks, that animals do so constantly and undoubtedly read them much more often and more accurately than humans. Equally sad that he should also have reduced them to a single function: that of dirtying something in order to appropriate it.

There remains one further matter, to which I shall be returning later (since singing could be interpreted in a similar way): if the act of marking does indeed create the effects of presence in absentia, certain writers have suggested, notably with reference to the mountain goat or to certain animals in captivity, that marking also represents an extension of the animal's body in space.[25] In this context, the term 'appropriation' takes on another meaning, since here it is a matter of transforming the chosen space not so much into something the animal 'owns', something which belongs to it, as into the animal 'itself'. The distinction between 'self' and 'non-self' is even less clearly defined, in that many mammals not only mark locations and objects, but they also mark their own bodies with their own secretions, transferring these onto different parts of the body. More astonishing still, many of them also steep themselves in the smell of objects found within the area of the territory – soil, grass, rotting carcasses, tree bark. The animal then becomes appropriated both *by* and *into* the space which it appropriates as its own by marking it, thus creating a physical bond with that place which renders the 'self' and the 'non-self' indistinguishable.

It is clear that what we are looking at here is something much more complicated than the simple regime of appropriation described by Serres, and if I were to continue the list of such differences, interspersed with a few partial resemblances, it would be almost endless. But what I am trying to emphasize here is the fact that, when it comes to territories and what we can learn from them, there is no such thing as an 'all-purpose' approach that can be applied to every situation. Moving from one territory to another – whether it be that of a particular animal which is the focus of researchers' interest or that of scientific methods – cannot be undertaken just like that, without due precautions, without paying attention to the incredible diversity of modes of being which territories have helped to create. And this is also why I am keen to stress that certain ornithologists – not all of them, certainly, and we shall be returning to this later – very quickly understood that territories could not easily be encompassed by *one* general theory. In 1956, moreover, in his introduction to a special edition of the journal *Ibis* which was dedicated to territories, the British zoologist Robert Hinde wrote that 'the diversity of nature can never fit into a system of compartments and categories.'[26] Categories, he added, are only there to help us in our discussions. They are all the more questionable given that, within the same species, in the course of the same period of time, we can find very different practices, simultaneously or in sequence, and, in other species, we might observe practices which vary according to age, sex, habitat or population density.

All this is no coincidence. From the very beginning, ornithologists were brought face to face with the diversity of species and very quickly developed a comparative approach which rendered them attentive to the plurality of different organizational structures.[27] Comparative approaches require, and encourage, a genuine culture of tact, a heightened attention to differences and to specificities, and a concern for what matters. It is a culture that many of them – not all, but those who turn out to be the most interesting – have learned to respect.

But it is, moreover, equally possible that something is happening in relation to territorial behaviour, a behaviour which, as I pointed out, left researchers astonished and moved. Very often birds demonstrate such vitality, such power of determination, such an outpouring of energy, in fact seem so utterly 'possessed' by what they are in the process of defending, that it would not be unreasonable to assert that researchers have themselves been touched by the sense of something which was *truly important*! And that this importance mattered.

Counterpoint

> Imagination, because it is a form of hospitality . . . enables us to welcome
> that which, in the feeling of the present, whets an appetite for otherness.
> Patrick Boucheron, *Ce que peut l'histoire*[1]

If there are territories which are bound by song, or, more precisely, territories which *insist* on being sung, if there are territories which are bound by the power of a simulacrum of presence, territories which become bodies and bodies which expand to become living spaces, if there are living spaces which become songs or songs which create a space, if there are forces of sound and forces of smell, there are undoubtedly many other ways of being, many other ways of inhabiting a territory, all of which may give rise to many different worlds. What verbs could we find to evoke these forces? Might there be danced territories (the power of dance to bring together)? Loved territories (territories bound by love? The power of love), disputed territories (bound by contention), shared, conquered, marked, known, recognized, appropriated, familiar territories? How many verbs might there be and which verbs constitute a territory? And what practices will enable these verbs to proliferate? I am convinced, along with Haraway and many others, that this multiplication of worlds can make our own world a better place to live in. Creating such worlds means learning how to respect different ways of inhabiting a given space, identifying and itemizing what animals do and how each of them has developed its own way of being. This is what I expect of researchers.

I use the term 'inhabiting', but in fact 'cohabiting' would be a better term, for there are no ways of inhabiting which do not first and foremost mean 'cohabiting'. And I use the word 'itemizing' because this is intentionally the most modest project I have been involved in, one requiring me simply to list 'habits', and by that I mean not routines but, rather, the inventions of life and the practices which link action and knowledge to places and to other beings. A project which involves investigating this subject, rethrowing the dice, describing with curiosity what inhabiting generates in terms of relationships and of the different ways of being 'at home'.

In short, it is a matter of opening up the imagination by honouring inventions of all kinds.

I am not, however, looking to animals for enlightenment, and nor is it my intention to use them to find solutions to our problems. I have learned, and I am learning all over again with Serres, that, when we involve animals in this kind of operation, the very way the problem is formulated and presented ends up excluding those interrogated because it requires them to reply in terms already set out in advance. We will remember the embryologist Heape and his sweeping use of the term 'all animals', which already set alarm bells ringing, as did that other convenient short cut which enabled him conveniently to leap from animals to the whole of civilization. It is certainly no coincidence that, where territories are concerned, whenever the transition from animals to humans is made too rapidly, we find ourselves attributing to animals our own conception of territory as property. Our task should be to multiply worlds rather than to reduce them to our own. And to avoid insulting the practices which are part of this multiplication. Because these are indeed an important component of this process of multiplication, if only because they force us to be less precipitous about such transitions and to acknowledge their complexity.

Not surprisingly, then, I cannot help feeling irritated all over again when I read another example of the 'one size fits all' approach, this time in the analysis of some scientific research included by the sociologist Zygmunt Bauman in his book *Does Ethics Have a Chance in a World of Consumers?*.[2] The opening pages of this book describe an important discovery relating to social insects and to what constitutes 'home' for certain wasps – the reason why I had been urged to read it. According to an article in *The Guardian*, Bauman writes, a group of researchers from the Zoological Society of London who had been studying local wasps in the Panama region came back with news that would astound anyone already familiar with the behaviour of social wasps. They had made a discovery that they claimed would overturn the centuries-old stereotypes concerning the social habits of these insects. Zoologists had always thought that wasps confined their sociability to their nests, or, in other words, to the community into which they had hatched and to which they belonged. This notion was so widely accepted that scientists had for a long time dedicated a considerable amount of research to investigating how the insects successfully identified strangers and then either forced them to leave or killed them. Was it by sound, by smell, or by behaviour? 'The intriguing question', Bauman writes, 'was how the insects managed something that we humans, with all our smart and sophisticated tools and weapons, only half succeed in achieving – that is, how they kept the boundaries of their "community" watertight and maintained the separation between "natives" and "aliens", between "us" and "them".'[3] The scientists discovered, however, that in fact a significant majority (56 per cent) of working wasps change nests in the course of their lives, and that they integrate fully with their adoptive community, participating in collective work. This discovery turns out to be linked to cutting-edge technology that enabled certain wasps to be fitted with a small radio system which was attached to their thorax. Each time a tagged wasp entered or left, this would then trigger an electronic sensor situated at the entrance of each nest.

If Bauman mentions the role of this new technique in what he describes as a reversal of perspective, he nevertheless points out that this is not the most significant element here. What was most significant, he says, was the fact that, before this, nobody had thought of investigating this aspect and that we think about it now precisely because, and I quote again, 'these scholars of a somewhat younger generation brought to the forest of Panama their own experience (and ours) of the life practices acquired and absorbed in their newly multicultural home of interlocking diasporas.' And as a result, Bauman continues, 'they duly "discovered" the fluidity of membership and perpetual mixing of populations to be the *norm* also among social insects.'[4] In short, 'beliefs that not so long ago were imagined to be reflections of the "state of nature" have been revealed now, retrospectively, to have been but a projection onto the insects' habits of the scholars' own human, all-too-human, preoccupations and practices.'[5] Which also means, and Bauman himself makes this point, that discoveries made by scholars depend above all on the modifications of beliefs and of 'the "conceptual nets" we have inherited'.

We cannot, of course, fail to agree with Bauman's assertion that new questions can emerge from a changing world. What, then, it might reasonably be asked, is the cause of my irritation? It is how these changes are presented that strikes me as profoundly questionable.

Let me first of all draw attention to a detail which seems to me an important one. Bauman, as I have already mentioned, gets his information from an article published in *The Guardian* newspaper, on 25 January 2007, which heralded the discovery.[6] The article does not mention the names of the researchers, but I had no difficulty in tracking down the relevant scientific publication, which had appeared just two days earlier.[7] Bauman had clearly failed to consult this article and based his evidence on the few lines published in the newspaper. In the scientific article, however, the researchers explain that they had conducted an initial experiment with these wasps in 2004, and that the evidence obtained on that occasion indicated that only 10 per cent of the wasps observed appeared to change nests. The research on which the current article is based dates from 2005 and, on the basis of these later findings, that figure goes up to 56 per cent. According to Bauman, between 2004 and 2005 the researchers therefore switched their cognitive framework. Except that the researchers explain that, in 2004, they used a traditional method which entailed marking a certain number of wasps from each nest with paint and monitoring any changes in living arrangements by noting which wasps were in each nest at various different times. The 10 per cent figure in fact corresponded to 100 hours of observations. In the knowledge that, as a result, many wasps would have changed nests without being observed, the researchers estimated, by extrapolation, the number of insects visiting other nests at 25 per cent. In 2005, however, with the aid of the new technique, the 422 wasps fitted with monitoring equipment represented 6,000 hours of observation. The researchers were adamant that, unless nests were observed continuously, the old method could not possibly hope to obtain results as high as those resulting from the technique involving electronic tagging. For Bauman, however, this change in the method of observation is not particularly significant. In his view, what matters in this case, what changes in terms of what is observed in the wasps, are the new cognitive habits derived from 'our novel experience of an increasingly and probably permanently variegated setting of human cohabitation'.[8] It is these new cognitive habits which enable us to envisage a concept which would hitherto have been impossible, namely the idea that wasps might indeed be capable of a far more hospitable lifestyle than had been previously imagined.[9] The fact that Bauman did not take the trouble to read the article written by the scientists certainly suggests a certain lack of curiosity. And a certain temerity, too, given that almost the entire introduction to his book is based on what he learned about the wasps in the dozen or so lines in *The Guardian*. It is not, however, this arrogance that bothers me but the kind of *ethos* which leads certain academics to feel 'at home' in any field whatsoever. And even that would not in itself be significant if it did not produce the effects of a certain mode of attention, or rather of inattention, of negligence even.

Bauman sets little store on the equipment, the binoculars, tags, chips, statistics, sonograms, notebooks, paint markings, wired-up nests – in other words, all the instruments which help make things visible, which establish connections, which bring an intimacy to our understanding and which throw light on similarities and differences, on trajectories and habits. All of that is apparently incidental: it is the ideas of the scientists themselves that are really important. Which means that the 6,000 hours of observation obtained as a result of 'remote monitoring', as opposed to the 100 hours of observation obtained through paint marking, enabling the percentage of wasps observed to move nests to increase from 10 per cent to 56 per cent, is a mere detail, nothing more than an adjustment of ideas. Bauman seems utterly indifferent to the fact that understanding differently means first of all understanding more, and, in the case of the wasps, it means having better evidence in the form of more equipment, an increased presence, a closer proximity, a much greater intimacy and more reliable follow-up. The wasps live, as we now know, in the world of Ideas.

Ideas matter, of course. They lead to specific questions, and what researchers observe *orientates* their interests no matter whether these are focused on wasps, baboons or birds. Researchers are, for the most part, aware of this. They know that what they discover is related to the questions *they* are asking. And this concern goes far beyond a simple desire to avoid anthropomorphism. When I state, as I have done, that warlike or competitive vocabulary results in a certain type of focus, it is because researchers have told me so themselves. When certain scientists advance the theory that the function of territory is to control population density (we will be returning to this in chapter 3), since only those who have established a territory are able to reproduce, others worry that this theory of demographic regulation might perhaps simply reflect our own concerns regarding overpopulation. When territorial behaviour in fish is described by some as being rigidly aggressive and violent, others point to the fact that the observations in question have been obtained in the very constrained space of an aquarium.

What Bauman neglects to take into account is that the equipment used in research constitutes an alternative way to interact with animals, an alternative way of creating a certain form of intimacy with them. And researchers are well aware that intimacy can only be achieved as a result of hard work. Margaret Nice is one of the most prolific and most interesting ornithologists in the field of research on territory. Initially she began studying territories as an amateur, observing song sparrows in the neighbourhood of her house in Ohio. She very quickly realized that it would be impossible to know and understand these birds unless she was able to recognize them individually. Consequently, at the end of the 1920s, she began to band birds with a combination of four coloured rings and one aluminium one. This technique of ringing or banding was not a new one. At the end of the eighteenth century, a monk called Lazzaro Spallanzani had come up with the idea of attaching coloured threads to birds' legs in order to verify the theory that some of them, observed to disappear at the end of the summer, might in fact migrate.[10] If the practice was not therefore totally unknown, it was nevertheless still little used and, until Nice adopted it, was reserved as a means of establishing migratory routes (or, moreover, of identifying domestic birds in order to prevent them being illegally traded). Nice had a very different objective in mind. For her, it was not a matter of establishing travel routes but, rather, a way of attributing biographies to birds in order to obtain a deeper understanding of what was important to them when they established their territories. In 1932, 136 sparrows, both males and females, were banded – even though in fact Nice knew the males so well that, in their case, she could tell them apart just by listening to them, since each had its own unique repertoire of six to nine different songs. As a result of the banding, she discovered that males return to the same territory each year, that some of them migrate – the ones she would refer to as the summer residents – and that others choose to remain for the entire year – the winter residents. The male bird 2M lived for nine years, and during these nine years remained in the same location. Between 1930 and 1934, he moved a short distance away, barely further than 50 metres, but returned to the original location in the following years. The females, on the other hand, were less consistent and sometimes even changed partners in the course of the season, in order to produce a second brood. Nice also noted that fights involve what she describes as birds 'assuming the role' of despot or underling. When a bird attempts to gain access to an occupied territory, he visibly adopts, in behavioural terms, the role of the invader: the closer he gets to the centre of the territory, the less determined he seems to be and the more aggressive the existing occupant becomes. In such a case, with reference to theories of hierarchy, it might be said that the resident takes a dominant role and the intruder adopts a subordinate role, and this corresponds to the difference in the intensity of aggressive behaviour. This explains why, in the case of song sparrows, changes of occupants within a given territory are rare. But what appears to represent a rule turns out in fact to be a somewhat more complicated matter. If, for example, the territory occupied the previous year by a migratory bird turns out to be already occupied on his return, it is the current occupant, the resident bird, who takes on the role of intruder. Except in rare cases, he will be driven out. The fights previously described between birds, Nice points out, make no mention of such differences of roles, probably because the birds were not banded.

The technique of banding made it possible to get to know life stories, attachments to particular places, birds capable of making choices. So, for example, bird 4M, who was banded in 1929 but who was suspected by Nice to have occupied the same territory in the previous year, remained in the same location, but would move a few metres each year. During the winter of 1931–2, he lived 30 metres further west, without any apparent opposition from other birds. In the early years, he was a combative bird, the neighbourhood tyrant. He constantly forced his neighbour, 1M, to defend his borders. From 1932 onwards, his energy for picking fights diminished, and he even allowed 110M, a young summer resident, to establish himself in the former territory of 1M without the slightest protest. In the course of the following winter, he moved even further west, into what had previously been the territory of 9M. He nested there for three years, before returning to the researcher's garden in 1935. As each bird was identified, Nice discovered that personal relationships were sometimes significant, which explained the fact that certain winter residents were sometimes tolerated on a territory in the process of being established and that, in situations where some kind of conflict might be expected, matters were sometimes settled in a different way, as in the case where a summer resident, returning from migration and finding a fellow bird already installed, clearly preferred to go elsewhere rather than chase off the intruder. Sometimes a change of territory occurs without any apparent pressure from other birds. Birds like routines, but also sometimes like to change them. During the same period, Barbara Blanchard was studying Nuttall's White-Crowned Sparrows in California. A family group consisting of three birds subdivided the territory into two sections, and each of these was exclusively occupied and defended by a single bird. There were endless disputes between these two birds and constant singing and fighting. Blanchard discovered, contrary to all her expectations, that both of these birds were females. And she wrote: 'Had they not been banded, I should have thought I was watching a boundary dispute between two males.'[11] And Nice noticed that, in the case of the song sparrows, the females learned the boundaries from their partners and generally accepted them. But in 1929, one of them, K2, built her nest in the territory belonging to 4M, a neighbouring bird (see above), creating, Nice remarked, considerable difficulties for her partner, 1M, until such time as he was able to annex that portion of the territory.

We might, of course, be tempted to digress here, and to attribute the interest these two researchers have in female birds to the fact they are themselves women. We might certainly be more inclined to imagine such a scenario in the case of Blanchard in that, throughout her entire career, she continued to be a victim of her status as a woman. The profession was very much a male-dominated one and there was clearly a keenness to keep things that way. When Blanchard proposed doing her doctoral thesis on birds, her undergraduate mentor suggested she should study worms instead, on the grounds that these are far more simple creatures. She held her ground and studied the behavioural differences and song dialects in white-crowned sparrows, differences which she would discover were linked to whether the birds were migratory or not. And when she applied for an academic post, she was informed that, if a man with the same qualifications were to apply, he would be given preference over her. The letter of recommendation given to her by her supervisor, when she was planning to visit a research site, mentioned only that she should be granted access because she was of a cheerful temperament. There are a great many such anecdotes, and Blanchard would recount them with humour in order, as she said, to draw attention to the absurdity of the era.[12] Nice's career followed a different path. Although she abandoned her thesis in order to follow her husband and take on the role as mother to their growing family, she nevertheless, and with remarkable obstinacy, continued for many years to observe birds as an amateur, in her garden and in the surrounding area, before an encounter with the biologist Ernst Mayr encouraged her to publish her findings and to allow her work to become known. But while these two different career paths do indeed represent the lot of women scientists in a rather bleak era, with one battling against academic male chauvinism and the other for years snatching whatever time was left available to her after a career of wife and mother to a large family, they cannot be simply reduced to this historical position. Firstly, both of them broke away from the prevailing habits in the field of ornithology, notably that of the classification of specimens, to focus instead on behavioural variations within the same species and sometimes within the same groups. Both of them were determined to follow individual and living birds because it was at this level that any differences were most evident and most significant. From that point on, females, apparently so often assigned a background role in the drama of territoriality, did not suddenly move centre stage because, as Bauman might for example have imagined, they were observed by women who had taken it upon themselves to investigate their role (Blanchard's surprise at seeing the female birds' involvement in this tells the opposite story) but because the bands had in fact made them *noticeable*. These bands are, therefore, devices aimed at focusing attention – or, in other words, devices enabling things which would previously have passed unnoticed to be seen.

In effect, as a result of those metal and coloured bands, other elements began to take on importance, new differences started to emerge, and these changed the way scientists would describe birds. Not only was it apparent that they had unique and individual lives, but they also became more flexible, more complex and capable of display-ing variation, as evidenced by behavioural ingenuity and unexpected tendencies within the same species. This is why such practices matter, since not only do they set in train a certain mode of attentiveness which allows differences to emerge, but also because they raise the question of what matters to birds, a question which, undisputedly in their case, makes them more interesting, and one to which the birds' own responses demonstrate a multiplicity of modes of being – summer resident, winter resident, male, female, intruder, resident, resident taking on the role of intruder, intruder taking on the role of resident, male tyrant subsequently calming down, distracted female, combative female.

It will be clearer from this that what I criticize in Bauman is this lack of curiosity typical of those who consider all fields to be a kind of 'home from home'. For him, the wasps, when all is said and done, are merely an indicator of our own social changes – this is what I mean by a 'one size fits all' hypothesis. And such an approach can only work by ignoring, whether deliberately or not, how we have obtained our knowledge of them, how other proposals for further study of them have been applied and the way the wasps respond to the proposals advanced by scientists – and provide the latter with what are sometimes new ideas. Nature is called on only to be ultimately silenced, with the declaration that anything we find there is merely the effect of our 'conceptual nets'. It will be of little surprise, then, that this absurd idea that nature is dumb still persists given that the only way of invoking it renders it mute.

In short, in the case of Bauman, as with Serres, everything advances at too rapid a rate. They forget that any perception of resemblances hinges on the active suspension of differences. Casting light on one situation by the illumination offered by another is a gesture which should be a matter of aesthetics and creativity. It requires taste, curiosity, tact, and some measure of duplicity. It is not a question of rejecting comparisons and analogies, of refusing to look for coincidences or convergences of interests but, rather, about trying to do all of that more attentively, of being careful about what connections are made and of acknowledging that there is a certain duplicity in claiming that whatever drew attention to the difference did not do so with sufficient force. In short, it is about taking care that, when new light is thrown on a situation, it does not then end up obliterating everything under the harsh spotlight of the explanation. Let us have softer, subtler lights instead.

2

The Power to Affect

In the space of just a few years, from the beginning of the twentieth century onwards, research on territory would suddenly take off. In her historical inventory of English-speaking countries, Margaret Nice lists eleven publications over the course of the first decade, fifteen in the second, forty-eight in the years 1920 to 1930, and 302 in the years 1930 to 1940. With these publications, theories would rapidly proliferate. By the time Robert Hinde published his survey, at the beginning of the 1950s, territory was associated with no fewer than ten different functions.

I am not going to tell this story by following a chronological thread. Instead, I would rather follow it as a history of ideas, of intuitions, of openings, for territories and birds have inspired people to think, and it is this which interests me. I opt therefore for a story constructed as a series of folds, one in which an idea is followed from the moment it first emerges, inspired by birds and taken up by a researcher, and then rediscovered as it reappears once more, hidden in other folds, when a writer, confronted with other birds, follows it up or stumbles upon it again, at a much later stage, as part of a different problem, and sometimes without even knowing that it had already, long before, been thought about by someone else. This works for certain ideas which develop into hypotheses and which go on to enjoy several different lives, or simply one very good one, when birds have succeeded in inspiring a researcher and convincing him or her that the theory in question touches on something of importance for them, something that may have mattered to others, to other birds and to other researchers who would follow in their footsteps. Or else, when ideas have led to controversies, because other birds were involved, and these insisted something different be taken into account. For some ideas, life will be more difficult, such as for example the notion that robins like solitude, an idea which failed to secure a champion and which I would encounter again, albeit in a somewhat different form, only in the final stages of my investigation. There is therefore an ecology of ideas associated with birds, one which is all the more interesting in that, as far as territories are concerned, it does not follow a regular trajectory in terms of progress. Many of the ideas are indeed present in the earliest research only to disappear temporarily through lack of support. There are hypotheses which have to wait until a bird comes along to challenge them, or until a scientist once again devotes his or her attention to them, and which will resurface when the conditions are once again favourable. And there are others which are so powerful and so incapable of coexisting in harmony alongside others that they end up invading and colonizing the entire domain, threatening to stifle all alternatives.

The story, as I have indicated, began before the twentieth century, even if the more ancient authors have only been allowed to participate retrospectively. This is the case of the German ornithologist Bernard Altum, whose work, dating from 1868, would be translated from German only in 1935. Altum asserted that the distances territories imposed between birds was a reflection of their greatest need: that of ensuring an adequate supply for the fledglings. All bird species have a special diet and, when seeking food for their young and for themselves – the single most important task for animals, according to Altum – will confine their movements to a relatively small area. They must not establish themselves near other couples because of the danger of famine and therefore require a territory of a given area, depending on how productive that area is likely to be. This idea persisted for a considerable time, even though fiercely debated and very often refuted. Henry Eliot Howard outlined it himself, unaware of the work of his predecessor. For him, the function of a territory was to provide a sufficient food supply. It also acted as a means of regulating population – only birds which had succeeded in acquiring a territory could reproduce, and this acted as a powerful limit on growth. For species living in colonies, such as seabirds for example, where there is unlimited access to food supplies but a shortage of nesting sites, the role of territory serves only this second function.

Population control and the need to guarantee a zone capable of providing an adequate supply of food can therefore be regarded as separate issues. I shall return to the theory of population control later but will concentrate here on the theory that territory guarantees the subsistence of those defending it. As has been pointed out, this hypothesis was the earliest one to be proposed and is mentioned in Aristotle, although without reference to the word 'territory'. It is easy to see the logic of this, provided we avoid focusing on the idea that animals 'own' a site over which they have exclusive use. If the territory is a nesting site, it is much more economical and safer for each couple to limit their movements. Moving away from the nest in order to find food and provide for the brood increases danger. Not only because the parent birds leave the fledglings unsupervised, with the result that predators, or even other birds of the same species where cannibalism is practised, might well take advantage of their absence, but also because doing so forces them to venture into less familiar terrain. The territory is therefore a familiar area which has the merit of providing a local food supply as well as being recognized as a site offering protection against predators.

From the outset, as Nice observes, this hypothesis failed to find unanimous approval. In 1915, John Michael Dewar was observing oystercatchers and noted that the borders between territories were often very flexible, depending in part on the presence or absence of other feeding couples. Each territory consisted of a zone for nesting and for the supply of food, but around this area a much more extensive feeding zone seemed to represent a 'common property' where all the birds from the surrounding area came to feed without danger.[1] The females of certain warblers, observed some years earlier by Sidney Edward Brock, would sometimes build their nests outside the territory of the males with which they were associated. In 1931, the ornithologist Lord Tavistock cast derision on what he called 'the great food shortage delusion' when, on a territory where he was observing a particular type of willow warbler, he found there was sufficient food to feed a dozen of the birds. Similarly, and I could quote numerous other examples, in 1933, David Lack, a British ornithologist, also observed that the most combative species in terms of territory did not appear to maintain strict territories while feeding their young. If it was a question of resources, he argued, then surely they would, on the contrary, be more aggressive at that time. In fact, he suggests, territory appears to be essentially a male issue, and its true significance seems to be in providing the male bird with a well-situated, prominent and isolated headquarters where he can sing or display. In 1935, Lack observed that, in the case of crimson-crowned bishop birds, passerines of the tropical regions, the female obtained her food outside the territory. The function of the territory would therefore probably be to isolate the male and to help the hens to find mates.[2] Still on the subject of the food supply function, Robert Hinde noted that the fact that a bird feeds on its territory does not mean that access to a food supply indicates any significant advantage, any more than a bird feeding outside its territory is proof that territory is unrelated to food supply.[3] Clearly the food supply function of territory is far from being universally accepted.

It is worth noting – and many researchers have pointed this out – that the hypothesis of territory as a food source would still, in spite of everything, continue to be relatively widely supported among scientists, notably because it was the least difficult one to study. Food-related behaviour is easily observed and measured. And it can be subjected to experimentation. If food supply is a major attraction in the choice of territory, the existence of an abundant source of food elsewhere, outside the territory, should cause birds to change location. Experiments carried out to this purpose would appear to suggest that food supply is not the determining factor since, in the majority of cases, birds accept the offer, go and feed elsewhere and then return to their own sites. But these experiments failed to have any real impact since few of them ended up being published, hence the persistence of this theory in spite of the many challenges to which it has been subjected. The explanation for this is simple and, according to Christine Maher and Dale Lott,[4] depends on the question asked: when researchers conducted experiments looking at the effect of changes of food supply on the way in which birds organize their space, they often ended up with negative results – no particular change occurred. Given that such results did not equip them to make any kind of claim, they would often end up not publishing them. Since only those who succeeded in demonstrating that this did indeed have an effect on social organization published their findings, a bias was therefore created in favour of research which could establish a correlation between food supplies and social organization.

As I mentioned earlier, David Lack challenged the hypothesis relating to food supply and suggested an alternative. Territory was, according to him, a strictly male affair and constituted a headquarters from which birds could display and sing. At an early stage, ornithologists stressed the importance of song in establishing a territory. So, for example, Bernard Altum suggested that the song enabled birds to signal their presence to each other and to fix the boundaries of their territory. He observed that fights generally started when the males were singing and that the song continued during the course of the battle. In 1903, Charles Moffat declared that the role of song was 'to advertise the presence in a certain area of an unvanquished cock-bird, who claims that area as his, and will allow no other cock-bird to enter it without a battle.'[5] But why such an elaborate song when a few notes would surely suffice? According to Moffat, the elaborate song constitutes an advantage, since only victorious birds sing. As a result, they are able to practise their song and therefore improve it. The skill of the 'battle-hardened' singer demonstrates the quality of his performance to all those in the vicinity and will therefore enable the most talented 'to be those with the longest record of success in life' – rather as though the song acted as an acoustic coat of arms indicating numerous victories. The more mediocre singers, on the other hand, 'are naturally afraid to start competition with them'. Moffat rejects the theory of sexual selection according to which the song would be a means of attracting females. For him, the song certainly fulfils a role of 'self-presentation', as the theory of sexual selection would have it, but it is addressed not to females but to other males, both as a means of 'advertising' the merits of the singer and as a warning – the song, well performed, should act as a deterrent against what would be a vain attempt to take on such a talented singer.

By looking at it from this point of view, Moffat in a sense pre-empted what would come to be known as the theory of honest signals. The bird asserts its merits and does so in a reliable way given that cheating is out of the question, since the song, an honest signal, is the result of long practice, involving time, skill and good health, or, according to Moffat, a past composed of numerous victories. Moffat would use a similar theoretical approach to interpret the brilliant plumage displayed by some birds. The colours are not, he says, destined to attract the attention of females, as the theory of sexual selection would suggest. Instead, they have evolved, and I use Moffat's term here, as 'war paint', a colourful warning to rival males. 'I wish to observe', he continues, 'that I never, to my recollection, saw a conflict between two brightly-plumaged birds, in which the bright feathers were not brought into prominence in some striking manner during the fray.' Many examples are cited, such as that of the ruff, 'whose decoration is really useful as a shield in his very celebrated battles.' And when we see these brightly coloured birds perched conspicuously on the tops of shrubs, 'does not each of them remind us of a bright little flag, put up – as it were – to mark that such and such an area is under such and such a dominion?' These colours are therefore the means by which birds communicate possession of a territory to other birds, and, Moffat points out, 'if they do not help a bird to win his plot of ground, they, at any rate, render his subsequent possession of it less liable to disturbance.'

Moffat's proposals take the form of two separate hypotheses and prepare the ground for two theoretical outcomes. On the one hand, as has been clearly demonstrated, songs and colours not only serve to draw attention to the bird but also act as a warning and therefore end up limiting conflicts. This is what led me to see in his suggestions an intuition similar to that which would later inspire the theory of honest signals. The honest signal can act as a regulatory force in conflicts in that, for example, singing is a reliable indicator of a bird's health. There is no need 'actually' to confront the bird, in the form of a fight, in order to find out what the outcome of this would be. In this way fights, doomed in advance to be lost and pointlessly costly in terms of energy or risks, can be avoided. It is important to remember that the question of aggressivity has, from the beginning of its history, been associated with territory, and that the matter of how this aggressivity might be controlled would be, notably for Konrad Lorenz, inextricably bound up with its emergence. Territory would be seen as the direct result of aggression, providing a means of controlling it by distributing animals across a given area, at an appropriate distance from each other. We shall return to this in the following chapter.

But, on the other hand, Moffat's idea that colours and songs might be primarily forms of self-promotion would lead some researchers to turn their attention to a very interesting question, notably the issue of appearances. What is emerging here hints at one of the most fascinating dimensions of territory, a dimension which would be explored in such an interesting manner by Gilles Deleuze and Félix Guattari in their book *A Thousand Plateaus: Capitalism and Schizophrenia*, in which they explore the idea that territorial behaviour is primarily an expressive behaviour. Territory is a *means of expression*. Or, in Étienne Souriau's words, territory, in the case of birds, with their colours, songs, displays and ritual dances, is permeated with *spectacular intent*.[6] Which also means that territory creates a certain kind of attention, or that it co-opts particular modes of attention: everything is territorialized, the one receiving the messages just as much as the one sending them. Together, a new kind of code comes into play.

But by asserting that territory is a means of expression, or a vehicle for spectacular display, I am drifting away from the notion that the function of this 'spectacularization' is to regulate fights by acting as a substitute for them. Because, if territory can indeed be defined as a spectacular display ground, aggressivity can no longer be the motive, in the psychological sense, or indeed the cause of territorial activity. It becomes instead the motive in an aesthetic or musical sense, conferring on the territory its style, its particular form, its energy, its choreography and its gestures so that aggression becomes a kind of simulacrum. There is a shift from an 'aggressive' function to a different function, an expressive one. Territorial behaviour adopts *the forms* of gestures associated with aggression, just as, in play, all the gestures of a fight – biting, threatening, chasing, hunting, etc. – are borrowed and turned into something else which has a very different meaning. Aggression as an expressive mode, like the gestures of animals at play, is akin to 'pretending': the gestures of play, like those associated with territory, abolish the materiality of the real, sublimate it, 'preserving only a pure form which has a value of its own', as Souriau writes. These are, for example, what he calls 'mimicries', such as when the rituals of threat, while in this 'pretend' mode, adopt the gestures of aggression. Later, he expresses regret that 'certain biologists interpret matters in too rationalistic a manner, seeing in this just a simple strategy to limit the dangers of combat: the same result, they claim, can be obtained through mimicry, but with less damage being done. But these two different approaches do not necessarily produce the same results. The winner is not the best fighter, but the best actor.[7] The notion that the aggression which appears to guide territorial behaviour might constitute a 'performance', the extravagant nature of which would moreover provide reliable evidence that this was indeed the case, had already been envisaged by certain researchers. We remember Nice and her intuition that these birds were 'assuming the role' in flexible and interchangeable ways. Nice would moreover write that, in the case of song sparrows, the more impressive the spectacle, the less serious the encounter was likely to be, a case of bluff substituting for action. I shall return to this in a later chapter, since this question has itself met a variety of different fates and has furnished researchers with a fascinating enigma: if everything is merely simulacrum and if, as some claim to be the case, the outcome of fights is so predictable, *Cui bono?* To what purpose?

But if I stay as close as possible to Moffat's proposals, it is clear that, in the context of territory, appearances become part of a new balance of power – the power or the magic of appearances capable of operating at a distance to preserve a distance. Such very particular modes of appearance as represented by songs as 'things intended to be heard'[8] and by colours and displays as 'things intended to be seen' were considered by Darwin as indications of the effect of sexual selection. Their role was to attract the attention of females, to seduce them. In return, the females exercised strong selective pressure in favour of certain traits, the most brilliant colours, the songs, the extravagant choreography. Moffat disagreed with this theory and was adamant that females had very little role in all of this. Other researchers followed in his footsteps, but without necessarily excluding the role of females. Some suggested that colours, songs and courtship displays were selected by females and were then redeployed in order to fulfil the territorial function of self-promotion. Others took the opposite approach, arguing that it was the existence of a territory that allowed these appearances to emerge and that these subsequently come to the notice of females, which, through the choices they subsequently made, exercised a selective pressure in favour of certain features. The different modes of appearance would, in each of these versions, become part of new combinations of forces, capable of operating other types of magic, of producing other effects – of fascinating, attracting, seducing, stimulating desire, creating an impression, frightening or imposing a distance.

Whichever one of these two narratives is favoured, appearances – or modes of appearing – are, from this perspective, *put to the service* of the power to affect. And if I emphasize the fact that they are 'put to the service', it is because these narratives open life stories up to new ways of inventing and reinventing roles and uses, to imaginative crafting, to expedients, to reinterpretations, to exuberant forms of opportunism. A case of throwing everything possible onto the fire, but what a fire! What splendour! 'To put it simply, the birds are singing much more than Darwin permits', wrote the Dutch biologist Frederik Buytendijk in 1932.[9] This, too, is another destiny of territory, a fragile destiny because little favoured by biologists, which is that of having succeeded in making some of them think that all forms of behaviour are not necessarily adapted or useful, but that, for example, 'birds are beautiful because they are beautiful to themselves.' Or even perhaps to advance the daring theory that those huge, vividly coloured feathers evolved simply to produce beauty – and it was only later that they were co-opted for the purpose of flight.[10] For these biologists, it is not a question of abandoning the idea that specific functions might have encouraged the adoption of certain traits or behaviours, the idea that evolution had some 'hold' on what might be considered useful. Looking for a function amounts to retracing a story, one that tells of the emergence of something new which will seek out a life, a being ready to welcome and embrace it and capable of making it into something, or 'something else', a being who will then enter into a new kind of relationship with the air, the temperature, with conspecifics, with the environment. And it is this 'something else' which must not be lost to sight. For, as Baptiste Morizot reminds us, the question 'what is it for?', to which we are sometimes tempted to reduce function, tends to obscure the fact that natural selection has in the past had an impact on a great many successive functions of one single trait, and that 'this heritage echoes with the murmurings of rich possibilities. The individual consequently has a certain margin of freedom when it comes to reinventing uses.'[11] This notion of 'uses' emphasizes the fact that, if animals do indeed inherit certain characteristics which have been selected because they were useful in a particular circumstance, these characteristics carry with them the memory of the multiple different uses with which they have been associated over the course of their history, the reinterpretations and the reinventions to which they have lent themselves. And these different uses remain available in order to create 'something else' from the same trait, feather, song or aggressive gesture and can even once again become part of the selection process, in a completely different context.

Turning our attention to Moffat once again, the hypotheses claiming that territories are primarily a male matter have sometimes been contested. It is true that, from a purely logical point of view, females should indeed have a role to play, since a great number of territories – the majority of them in fact – are associated with reproduction. But it is also true that, in these various hypotheses, females seem always to remain in the background of the territorial stage, often restricted to the role of spectator or, at best, to a walk-on part, or even, in a great many cases, simply seen as a resource. With a few exceptions, however. In 1935, it was discovered that mockingbirds have two territories, one for summer and one for winter, the latter being a supply zone which is defended by both male and female birds. The female does not, however, defend the summer territory. That same year, the Dutch ornithologist Nikolaas Tinbergen discovered that, in red-necked phalaropes, it is the female who secures and defends the territory. She performs a ceremonial flight accompanied with mating calls directed at any new arrival. If the newcomer turns out to be female, she attacks her; if it is a male, she engages in courtship. A few females also stand out, some of them because they display territorial behaviour towards other females, others because they participate in fights alongside the males. In the ringed robins observed by David Lack at the end of the 1930s, the males defended a territory all year round, while females defended it only during the autumn. We may recall that Barbara Blanchard recorded that what she believed to be a fight over boundaries between two males in fact turned out to be fought by two females. Her initial error says a lot about what was to be expected of female birds. Very recently, three researchers, Katharina Riebel, Michelle Hall and Naomi Langmore, voiced their concern that nobody within the scientific community appeared to be interested in singing females. The title of their very short article speaks volumes: 'Female songbirds still struggling to be heard'. It would appear that singing is rarer in females than in males. Nevertheless, the authors point out, over the course of the last few years evidence has begun to suggest that female songbirds are more common than had previously been thought. And it would appear that, where females do sing, their songs are often highly complex, reflecting the effort required to learn them. Originally, these three writers suggest, both male and female songbirds would have sung. And nobody has the slightest idea as to why so many female birds might have stopped doing so.[12]

It remains the case nevertheless that, in the current literature on the subject, territory is still largely a male domain. But given that, from the emergence of the very first theories, territory was seen as a vital element in the reproductive process, at some point or other, females must have a role to play, no matter how small that role turns out to be. For certain scientists, including Howard, the role of territory would be to provide a meeting site. Its function, according to him, would even be to ensure 'freedom of movement for each individual'. Howard proposes an imaginary scenario[13] according to which certain birds only construct their nest a short time after pairing. If the couple do not have a territory, there will be a period of time between pairing and the construction of the nest, an interval during which both male and female will wander freely, guided only by the search for food. In this case, any reunion between the couple will be completely a matter of chance, given that they will have no shared space in which to meet, nothing to attract them to each other and nothing to detain them in any one place. However, if the disposition of the male bird leads it to establish a territory, each one is free to come and go and even to associate with other individuals without the risk of permanent separation, and is therefore sure to be able to find the other when the time to build a nest arrives.

Similarly, when couples remain stable from one season to the next but live together only during the reproduction season, females can more easily find their partner, provided he has returned to the same site as the previous year, as is the case with many birds. The function, or effect, of territory would therefore be to ensure links were in place to attach the males to the territory, the females to the males. It represents, in a sense, the invention of conditions of attachment. Some would see territory as a means of facilitating encounters, given that it provided the security necessary for the coupling rituals to take place. These are often long processes, which require very delicate adjustments – and it is not impossible that displays and songs form part of the rituals through which the male stimulates the female, even possibly synchronizing the reproductive cycles.

Furthermore, territory offers the female protection from the tentative approaches of other birds. This is, for example, the case with the song sparrows, described by Nice as particularly incorrigible in this respect: 'the male Song Sparrow has the habit of "courting" in his peculiar rough way, neighbouring females in the temporary absence of their mates. Territory seems to be a temperamental necessity as well as an economic one.'[14]

Certain scientists would seek to expand the theory of sexual selection by suggesting that females might perhaps choose a particular territory rather than just a male. Their choice would then be determined by the qualities that territory had to offer. In turning their attention to this possibility, those scientists would first observe that the size of territory and the choice of matrimonial arrangement – monogamy or various forms of polygamy – were linked. So, for example, in a certain hummingbird species, the fiery-throated hummingbird observed in Costa Rica, the male establishes a territory. This will then be visited by females coming to forage there. These will be chased off, only to return again, until they succeed in mating with the male bird. The male, at this point, tolerates them. Provided, that is, that they do not feed on the nectar of flowers he has reserved for his own exclusive use. But he will nevertheless defend the flowers the females have chosen as their food supply against other birds. This prompts the authors to formulate the hypothesis that females are not so much choosing a male as a certain quality of territory. This is not at odds with sexual selection, since this includes all those characteristics that might be significant in the choice of partner. 'Territories [from this perspective] are externalized secondary sexual characteristics much as are the constructed bowers of bower birds', observe Larry Wolf and Gary Stiles.[15]

In the early 1960s, Jared Verner observed two groups of long-billed marsh wrens in Washington state, one in the Seattle region, the other a few kilometres away, near the town of Cheney, at Turnbull.[16] In view of the fact that certain birds opt for polygamy and others do not, Verner sets out to understand the reasons behind these choices in relation to different types of territory. The two populations studied differed in a number of ways. For example, in Seattle, males fed the young throughout the season, whereas at Turnbull they did so only at the end of the season. Many males, though not all of them, both in Seattle and at Turnbull, were polygamous, which meant that some of them would remain unmated in spite of the fact that they had their own territory. The females would base their choice on the quality of the territory and would therefore, in some cases, find themselves cohabiting a territory with others who had made the same choice. I will note in passing that, if this is the case, male polygamy would not, as is often suggested, be simply a 'male' strategy but would instead be the result of females choosing to cohabit with several others sharing the same partner. Among the bigamous males in Seattle, it was observed that the cycle of two females was aligned so that there were fewer than two days of overlap in their nesting period: when the first brood began to leave the nest, the eggs of the second brood were starting to hatch. Each female therefore benefited from the exclusive care of the male during almost all the nesting period. On the other hand, at Turnbull, males help with feeding only at the end of the season, and this synchronization was not observed. Verner assessed the quality of the different territories and concluded that the surface area of the territory was not of significant importance; what mattered was the quality of what was to be found there. The Turnbull females, by attaching themselves to a male living on a superior territory and by sharing him with another female, would therefore be choosing less help than if they had opted for an inferior territory inhabited by a single male. But some clearly chose this latter option, which explains why the marsh wrens are not all polygamous. On this subject, Verner refers to Male 25, whose site, although superior in terms of surface area, did not have much vegetation capable of providing cover, which clearly proved to be a determining factor for females. This male, he recalls, would prove to be less successful in courting and would only just manage to pair at a late stage. 'When he finally paired, the breeding nest was placed so precariously that I tied it firmly in place to prevent its dislodging.'

I would like to pause for a moment to look more closely at this anecdote. Something important is happening here which tells us that not all practice has succumbed to the conventions currently adopted in the sciences, conventions which require distance and indifference towards whatever is being observed, or which ban certain types of interference – a very relative or very partial ban, as we shall see later on. I was tempted, and this was my initial reaction, to say that Verner's behaviour demonstrates all the signs of an amateur. But that would mean neglecting the fact that, in the case of birds, some amateur practices have entailed undeniable violence – read Jean Rolin's magnificent novel *Le Traquet Kurde* [The Kurdish Wheatear] for an idea of what being a 'bird lover' can also entail. In the nineteenth century many amateurs were collectors, and there is every indication that, for some of them, love and appropriation amounted to one and the same thing. What Verner's approach testifies instead, if we are to avoid analogies which might prevent us from noticing jarring elements in similarities, is a particular form of attentiveness. And I cannot resist intuitively associating this careful and attentive approach with the attitude he brings to his research. It is an approach which focuses on differences. By being attentive to these differences, to the things which matter, the researcher is moved by what matters to birds. Admittedly, in this case, the practice in question is in the context of a theory which sets out to explore a vast issue – the choice of polygamy – but it seeks to explain that choice by actively taking account of *these* particular wrens, with their individual choices, illustrating how the differences between them give an indication of how each one, faced with the various possible options, endeavours to organize things as well as possible. Or sometimes less well. And all of this creates stories, real stories, daily adventures of real lives, of actors firmly endowed with good intentions, of plans and desires. Take for example the case of Male 16, who arrived in the marsh on 2 April 1961, some considerable time after other males had established their territories. He initially moved into an unoccupied area but soon afterwards began to challenge Male 2, whose mate was about to lay. Hounded, and hampered by the constraints of the situation, Male 2 was forced to give up part of his territory and to retain only a small segment of it. Male 16 found himself with almost the whole territory, including the area where the nest was located. 'This was the only occasion', writes Verner, 'on which a newcomer evicted an established male from his area of major activity, suggesting that Male 16 was more aggressive than normal.' With the enforced defection of Male 2, the female remained with Male 16, probably because she was on the point of laying and her nest was already lined. But once the nesting cycle was completed, she abandoned the territory and went off to join a third bird, who had remained unpaired up until then, probably because his territory was of relatively poor quality. This was one of the very rare cases, Verner points out, where a female changed mates while the original mate was still alive. But, he wrote, 'Perhaps Male 16's abnormally aggressive behaviour caused his abnormally acquired mate to desert him [abnormal because he had usurped the place of the resident already paired], indicating that he might never have acquired a mate had he established himself in the marsh at the beginning of the season when other males were not paired.' I have already mentioned, with reference to Isabelle Stengers, that knowing something could also be to some extent a question of taste. And it is probably this, more than simply the fact that Verner was contravening the scientific codes by getting involved and interfering in order to help the hapless bird, which initially made me view his approach as that of an amateur – the approach taken by those who 'love' and who develop a passionate expertise. Such behaviours are rooted in taste. The analogy with amateurs is too strong if it ends up obliterating the fact that, for amateurs who were bird collectors, love was neither a romantic affair nor an innocent relationship. Yet the analogy holds if we consider that, on the one hand, amateurs themselves have changed, and their behaviour towards birds has also gradually begun to change. And, on the other hand, it holds even more firmly if we read Verner's stories of wrens as evidence of the good taste of those who (like amateurs of music, of wine, or of anything that becomes a matter of taste simply as a result of being loved) seek out the minuscule differences that matter, are moved by these differences, and cultivate the art of making them count.

Let us return to the various hypotheses. A great many authors would also suggest that another function of territory would be to protect birds from predators. The bird knows the area, is familiar with it and therefore knows where it is possible to hide – a scenario we referred to above in connection with wren 25, whose territory had the disadvantage of failing to provide any cover. It also offers, as we have seen, protection against interference by birds of the same species, albeit a relative one, as the male and female who were victims of the intrusion of Male 16 clearly illustrate. This protective function of territory has often been evoked in the context of competition (for females or for resources). But, in the late 1940s, the ecologists of the Chicago school, under the leadership of the zoologist Warder Clyde Allee, would propose a much broader hypothesis. This reflected their interest both in the life of communities and in the relationships of interdependence which such 'assemblages' create and maintain, and also in the way animals subjectively experience their lives. Researchers, he writes, tend to focus on certain incidents: 'Dramatic incidents occur, and there is a strong tendency to record and to over-emphasize these. Animals, under many conditions, and plants as well, may merely persist; . . . The quiet retirement of animals capable of extreme activity is often a fundamental part of living.'[17] That tendency, incidentally, provokes the authors to condemn experimental practices, for 'an observer frequently has nothing to do except wait and watch. In fact, patience is one of the prime prerequisites for naturalistic study of undisturbed wild life, even when attention is limited to selected birds or mammals. The essential impatience of observers is one of the dominant reasons for the growth of experimentation in ecology.' If tranquillity is seen as a crucial dimension of animal life, territory would therefore play an important role, since it would provide not only a protected zone but also a place in which to mark a pause in between periods of intense activity. The authors explain that continuous activity within a community would be excessively demanding and would eventually lead to exhaustion and death. 'Periodic recuperation is usually accompanied by relative inactivity, and in this condition the animal seldom responds as rapidly or completely to external stimuli . . . Rest and sleep, or their physiological equivalents, are consequently generally consummated within a more or less sheltered place.'

From this perspective, and somewhat paradoxically given the agitation that can sometimes reign there, territory becomes a quiet place away from collective life, a place of retreat. Yet surely the paradox stems, in part at least, from the attention researchers pay to such agitation? Territory can provide a zone of partial disconnection from the demands of social life, a truce in the course of which other habits develop, protected by the behavioural conventions imposed by borders as well as by the 'roles' described by Margaret Nice. In short, a zone of tranquillity. Indeed, the notion that territory might be linked to matters of comfort, to predictable patterns and habits, was raised by Nice herself. Territory, she declared, was above all a matter of habit. The banding of birds demonstrated that many birds returned to their winter quarters, whether under normal conditions or when they were deported for experimental reasons. She cites Frank Fraser Darling, the British ornithologist and ecologist, who wrote in 1937:

Conservatism of habit, a factor of importance for the survival of species, tends to restrict movement to a particular area . . . Choice is another reason for individuals or groups remaining on one area. *Animals live in definite places because they like them.* Familiarity with one piece of ground enables an animal to use it in the most advantageous manner for its comfort and well-being.[18]

And, as Nice observes, we are ourselves familiar with such habits, with our tendency to sit in the same place at school, in church or in a public library. This idea of attachment to place is an unusual one in this field, since scientists generally tend to take a rather severe view of such notions. Nevertheless, in the work of Allee and his colleagues the Chicago school scientists, I find elements of something similar. They draw attention to the fact that very often animals migrate not as a reaction to a specific danger, but because they become aware of signals which they perceive negatively. 'Whether in this behaviour we can discern feelings akin to aesthetic feelings or whether they are to be looked upon as mechanical aspects of mental balance cannot be decided.' A few lines further on, they add that, although it is indeed important to be attentive to the risks of anthropomorphism, it seems to them unfortunate to have to use a Greek or Latin root meaning 'loving' in order to describe an ecological relationship (like philopatry) – 'when the English form would be objectionable or ridiculous.'[19]

A great many other versions of what territory might represent for birds could also be cited. As research continues, other territories will emerge, and these will take other forms and serve other purposes and other conventions.

The possibility of finding one single theory seems even more uncertain given that variations are multiplying, not only between species, but within the same species in different habitats. And sometimes even within the same species sharing the same habitat, as we have seen in the case of wrens. So, for example, Australian magpies can live in stable territorial groups of between two and ten individuals, where a maximum of three couples may reproduce, although a sub-species in Western Australia forms groups of up to twenty-six individuals, including six males who have opted to be polygamous.[20] In Australian magpies, differences occur between one group and another. The Scottish ornithologist Robert Carrick, who studied these birds in Australia in the late 1950s, recorded four different organizational types on the same site. He observed the permanent groups which were well established in vast territories with an abundant food supply. Other 'marginal' groups occupied inferior zones. He noted that there were also 'mobile' groups, which moved between feeding zones and nesting sites, and 'open' groups, which gathered on pasturelands and slept in a forest about a kilometre away. The latter are not territorial, do not nest, and are made up partly of birds formerly in a group but now separated from it – the loss of a dominant male in a group often results in the group breaking up. It was observed that, among the females of the non-territorial groups, the ovocytes do not develop.

The mobile groups are capable of producing eggs, but there is a poor survival rate among the young. The parent birds, forced to go further away to feed, leave them unsupervised and they often fall victims to predators in the form of crows, falcons or, according to the authors, to immature *Homo sapiens* who steal the young to raise as pets. A final characteristic of these groups is that mortality rates not only affect the families of permanent groups and of mobile groups differently but also vary depending on territoriality itself. In the course of the cold, wet winter of 1956, a form of tuberculosis killed many birds. As this was spread by contact, it did not kill any territorial birds, whereas, the author points out, at the height of the epidemic, dead birds from the open groups were collected on a daily basis. This succinct description suggests the possibility that a number of different functions are associated with territory: the death of magpies with only weak territorial associations supports the view of David Lack and many others, who believe that a territory, because it establishes distances, can offer protection against parasites and other carriers of disease. The apparent success of stable territories demonstrates that they offer a real economy of means in the search for food – this function may not be the only one, but clearly access to a territory makes life easier. It allows a social life to be established and favours physiological developments which then allow reproduction to occur.

Other researchers have reported observations of shared nests. The defence of the territory, a collective one in this case, is a matter neither of sex nor of food supply, but serves to protect a zone of land which in essence constitutes the extension of the nesting site.

Territories are multiplying. As new discoveries gradually emerge, other territories appear, and I am no longer referring here to other hypotheses, or other perspectives, but to other *territories*, other ways of inhabiting and therefore of existing alongside each other. As more research becomes available, habits – and I am referring to those of birds – become more and more divergent. This divergence is all the more dramatic in that habits are themselves modified by circumstances, that birds have very different life journeys, and that these journeys can not only favour the emergence of new functions but also sometimes preserve habits established by previous generations. All of which means that the choice of territory is not necessarily evidence of optimal adaptation to the situations with which we are familiar. So, for example, great tits have evolved in the primeval forests of Nordic countries and have been subjected to a powerful selective pressure given the high number of predators. With the gradual fragmentation of forests, the predators have largely disappeared. In many sites the installation of nesting boxes has considerably increased the density of great tits. Yet there is nothing to suggest that they choose their territories on the basis of what certain theories might suggest, such as food supplies for example, and we could just as easily suppose that they continue to be guided by indirect indications of a reduced risk of attack by predators.

Robert Hinde, as I have mentioned, reached the conclusion that it was impossible to reliably attribute any specific function to a given territory. We cannot in the end, he added, hope to understand the role of territory for any particular birds without a detailed knowledge of their life stories. Referring to this last comment, the American ethologist Judy Stamps notes that these conclusions, although undoubtedly pertinent, have discouraged field scientists and theorists from trying to formulate a global theory on these functions.[21] And, I would add, so much the better. Except that it is not altogether true.

Counterpoint

It is not altogether true for two reasons. First because, while it may be true in part (and only in part, as we shall see in the following chapter) with reference to the period dating from the beginning of the twentieth century to the end of the 1950s, a significant turning point occurred in the 1960s. Researchers had finally found a way of moving to a more generalized approach, thanks to economic theories. They applied these to a range of problems and were then able to calculate the costs and the benefits of each behavioural strategy and to present them in the form of a mathematical model. Such models were then produced with ever increasing frequency. Territorial strategies became a favoured subject. The act of holding or defending a territory was linked to costs in terms both of the amount of energy needed to protect it and to maintain its borders and of the behaviours associated with display and warning and the aggressive behaviour and risks involved in excluding rivals. The benefits were calculated with reference to the possibility of access to limited resources, which included females. By assigning the role of functions to these benefits (relating to food supply, reproduction or control of population density) and by attributing an estimated cost to each of these, the models made it possible to set out 'strategies which were stable from an evolutionary point of view' and therefore to mathematize the various individual stories. There are, after all, rules and laws in all of this. It will at last be possible to rid ourselves of this incorrigible diversity, these individual and ill-disciplined lives, the circumstances which upset the general picture and the worrying appetite displayed by living creatures for variations of all kinds. A universal converter, in the form of economics, now exists, and territories can at last be confined within a unified theoretical framework.

But, if we are to sound like economists, there is also a price to be paid. The first aspect of this, which will no doubt be regarded as anecdotal, is that the task of reading articles has become an extremely punishing one. A mass of figures, equations and graphs. Animals are not entirely absent in that they generally make an appearance towards the end of the article. When the equations of the various models have demonstrated what would appear to be the most reasonable choices, some animal or other is produced to say, yes, that is indeed how things are done. And, on this occasion, they really do remain very much in step. But perhaps I am drawn more to stories than to numbers, and maybe I am not sufficiently susceptible to the beauty of graphs, to colourful pie charts and to the choreography of curves which set out costs and benefits. All of these leave me cold. Yet, at the same time, other things are being said and, more importantly, are *failing to be said*. For the price to be paid is not simply a matter of taste. It also involves an element of negligence. The price of such models, Bruno Latour explains, is one which demands that economic theories adhere to a recent belief according to which

the interest of the individual – nation-state, animal, human, it hardly matters – can be calculated in only one way, by placing the entity on a territory that belongs to it exclusively and over which it reigns with sovereignty, and by shunting to the 'outside' everything that must not be taken into account. The novelty as well as the artificiality of this type of calculation is well brought out by the technical term 'externalization' – a precise synonym for *calculated negligence . . .*[1]

These economic models which set out to codify how territories are organized nevertheless feature a generous 'blind-spot' of deliberate negligence, given that the majority of them concentrate only on food supply. So, as the researcher Judy Stamps observes, risks from predators were eliminated from any calculation, as was the role of parasites and a whole range of other things which might have been important. In both the resulting articles and the researchers' imagination, the result has above all been a considerable reduction in the number of factors which might motivate animals, including any social factors. With economic theories, the focus switches to the effects of competition between conspecifics. Neighbours, wanderers, intruders . . . all find themselves absorbed into an equation as factors contributing to the cost of defending a territory. It is worth pointing out at this stage that methods of observation very much encouraged this approach: aggressive behaviours are more noticeable and more visible as well as being more easily measurable, and this is not generally the case, or at least not without considerable difficulty, when it comes to the more subtle social benefits that those in possession of a territory could offer each other, sometimes actively, sometimes simply by just being there. It is, for example, much easier to count the number of fights in which a bird gets involved than to measure the effects neighbours might have on the capacity of that same bird to detect or eject an intruder who might represent a threat. In addition, a considerable amount of research takes place in the laboratory (this is particularly the case for fish, but birds have not completely escaped the same fate), in a confined space, where sometimes aggression is the only way an animal can cope with a situation which is beyond its control. Competition as a way of thinking also becomes all the more imperative given that territory is defined by the quality of its food resources. The calculation is therefore almost sown up in advance: if population density increases, the food supply diminishes – or, in other words, animals have no choice but to compete with one another.[2] And that rules out an observation which, given the potential for distancing that territories primarily seem to provide, had at a very early stage left some researchers somewhat puzzled: the fact that, paradoxically, territorial animals seem to seek out the presence of others. And that territory might just be one of the ways in which this need can be met. We will return to this at a later stage.

3

Overpopulation

The essence of territoriality is to regulate the number of winners
and divide the population into haves and have-nots.

Vero Copner Wynne-Edwards[1]

Economic theories, as I have pointed out, are not alone in attempting to reintroduce some order onto this unruly array of usages. Before these, there was indeed one particular theory which made no secret of its ambition to identify the ultimate reason why territories exist, their true function, independent of all the various other functions they could support. And, to put it as succinctly as possible, this theory sought nothing less than to have the last word on the subject.

The theory of population control, demographic control, or control of population density appeared at a very early stage, though without the all-embracing nature it would later acquire. Moffat was the first to propose it. According to him, territory divides a given space into separate parcels in such a way that, at some point, all of these parcels end up being shared out between birds:

> And, once that happy state was arrived at, the number of nesting pairs each year would be exactly the same, the number of nests and the average number of young birds reared would be exactly the same; and whether there was a large mortality in winter, or a small mortality in winter, the total number of birds in the country would remain exactly the same.[2]

Darwin's notion of the great tragedy of the struggle for survival, which would explain the relative stability of populations, would require, according to Moffat's calculation, a mortality rate of 90 per cent in young birds before reaching breeding age. If such mortality rates might indeed be envisaged in the case of cannibal fish or in prolific breeders such as insects, they are far less plausible when it comes to birds. Moffat observed a colony of house martins over a number of years. He noticed that the number of birds returning in spring each year was practically the same as the number which had departed in the autumn. The famous perils of migration, he says, are 'altogether spasmodic'. There might indeed be a destructive storm or a hard winter, but such events do not occur with the frequency needed to prevent birds from increasing their numbers according to a geometric progression. Other restrictive factors must therefore be at work, and, Moffat writes, even if little is known about this process, 'I say we ought not to accept an unverified assumption that they always work by *killing*.'[3] By giving it the status of a metaphor, Darwin certainly relativized the concept of the *struggle for life*, but he failed to take into consideration that what was slowing down geometric growth in animals was the fact that many animals live 'the lives of old bachelors and old maids'. It had been assumed that birds fought each other over females, but why would this be the case if they were always guaranteed to find one, given that there were as many females as males and that apparently, according to Moffat, one mate is as good as another? But it is an altogether different matter if it turns out that the outcome of the fight was 'to prevent the defeated bird from rearing a family in the neighbourhood at all'. 'Birds may, or may not, realise the importance of protecting their future families against the ills of congestion', but, 'as land is a limited commodity, the cock birds in spring have to fight one another to settle the question.' After each of these battles, the loser is driven away and his matrimonial prospects are destroyed: 'It is not that he can't find a mate, but that he has no home to offer her.' I should stress in passing that Moffat's proposals already contain the germ of this manifestation of a lack of differentiation which will characterize the theory of population control – a model which applies equally to all situations, from then on rendered 'undifferentiated' as a result of his assumptions. Take, for example, the fact that one female is 'quite as good as another' in the eyes of a male bird, or the notion that the proportion of males and females is identical, a claim which is only theoretically true and, given that mortality affects the two sexes differently, often contradicted by the facts. And if land can indeed represent a limited commodity, this is not the case everywhere.

Howard would propose a similar hypothesis, though somewhat less fancifully. But enthusiasm for the proposition reached its peak with the theory expounded by Konrad Lorenz in his book *On Aggression*.[4] Lorenz starts by examining the question (alluded to in the German and French title though not in the English one): how can something as apparently evil as aggression in fact be a good thing? If aggression plays a perfectly understandable role in the relation between prey and predator, we might nevertheless question why it is also present in relationships between members of the same species. According to Lorenz, the primary function of aggression is to ensure the distribution of individuals in a given space in order to avoid overexploitation of resources. If a certain number of doctors and bakers were seeking to make their living in a particular region, they would be well advised to set up as far as possible from each other. The same is true of animals occupying a given space, where it is to their advantage if they are spread as evenly as possible across the available inhabitable area. The danger that, in any given part of the available biotope, too dense a population of a single species of animal could end up exhausting the food supply is eliminated in the simplest possible manner by aggression. In the hypothesis proposed by Lorenz, therefore, aggression acts to regulate distance and to control the distribution of individuals within a given space. This process of distribution results in territoriality.[5] Certainly, aggression is a dominant force, but, as Lorenz emphasizes, a great many different mechanisms are in place to channel and 'civilize' it. These include, in particular, displays and rituals, threatening behaviour which allows fights to be delayed or might even act as a substitute for them, and the possibility of diverting aggression into other channels, of reorientating or inhibiting it.

This theory certainly proved to be an immensely attractive one for a number of reasons. Its unifying power must certainly have been persuasive given the regrettable diversity of motives attributable to birds. It also had another advantage, enthusiastically seized on by researchers, in that it was easy to test by carrying out experiments. So, for example, if it could be demonstrated that, when male birds were removed from their territory, others quickly appeared to replace them and in turn eagerly embarked on the adventure of perpetuating the species, that would be proof that a considerable number of unmated birds were excluded from reproduction in order *to conserve resources*, at the same time constituting a reserve in case of extreme conditions and a high rate of mortality. This notion would moreover tally with the deeply entrenched idea that the strongest are favoured by selection, since they alone are given carte blanche to pass on their genes. And it also fits in with a competitive vision in a world with limited resources. But limited by whom? How? Where? The late nineteenth-century Russian naturalist Pierre Alexandre Kropotkin had already demonstrated that the limitation of resources and overpopulation was not a universal problem in the natural world, and that these constituted a constraint only in certain very precise circumstances.[6] In spite of innumerable cases demonstrating that this is not how it works, that selection has in fact more than one trick up its sleeve, and that there are indeed many areas in which it plays no role, the idea that territory is selected in order to avoid overpopulation still holds sway, however surprising that may be when, to say the very least, the notion has been widely refuted by the facts.

If birds avoid overpopulation on a *local* scale, it does not necessarily mean that they do so more *generally*. Over a number of years Dutch researchers studied the density of several species of tits in the Netherlands.[7] They observed that, from one year to the next, numbers remained constant on given sites, even though there was a surplus of nesting sites and food supplies varied from year to year. Once a certain number of birds had established themselves, subsequent arrivals would choose to settle elsewhere, in a less favourable but less densely occupied site. David Lack cited the example of great tits. He noted that mortality within the nest is low and more often occurs when there is a shortage of resources – caterpillars in this particular case – often corresponding with the arrival of a second brood. In such circumstances the young birds are hungry and make a lot of noise, and this attracts predators. Lack's calculation is a simple one: on the basis of twelve to thirteen eggs being laid per couple and per year, population growth should be 600 per cent. However, no growth is observed over the long term. Furthermore, the limits in terms of density are often exceeded. According to Lack, population is controlled by food resources rather than by territory, and only at a later stage, when the young birds are starting to be independent. At *this particular moment* only, and not at others, mortality due to a lack of resources is a decisive factor.

Many researchers have also challenged the theory of overpopulation because it failed to take into account a highly significant observation, notably the fact that birds clearly group their territories together. Why not scatter them more widely? One possible answer was of course that the most attractive sites attract the greatest numbers. But it appears that this is not always the case and that birds might be guided by other reasons. By focusing on the problem of overpopulation, there is, according to Warder Clyde Allee and his ecologist colleagues from Chicago, a tendency to forget that under-population can be just as critical for certain animals. It is no coincidence that Allee should pay particular attention to this aspect, given that throughout his work he focused on the way the life of each living creature or organism depended on that of others, in an 'ecological assemblage' which he also referred to as 'a community of living beings'. Such terms emphasized the fact that, in such assemblages, all organisms play a crucial role as the condition of existence for others – what Allee would call 'facilitation' or 'proto-cooperation'. All the individual elements within a community, living or dead, from the bacteria which have made respiration possible or which replenish the fertility of the soil to 'the rain of dead organisms from the surface of the ocean that permits the development of life in the great lightless depths of the sea',[8] associate in 'proto-cooperations'. Indeed, Allee borrowed from Darwin the notion of the 'web of life' and the example Darwin used to illustrate the most unexpected importance of one being for another in a cascade of interdependence. Darwin had observed that there was a relationship between the number of cats and the number of clover plants in an area adjoining a certain English community, an area where cats hunted field mice. The field mice were the predators of a certain species of bumble bee which nested underground. The bumble bees in their turn pollinated clover plants in the area. This meant that, the more bumble bees there were, the more clover there would be, and there would be more bumble bees as long as cats continued to thwart the habits of field mice. It is of course possible to broaden this community and investigate the presence of old maids who like cats, and eventually, through a whole network of stories, further explore the presence of these old maids by looking at the relationship between their numbers and the differential survival of men, etc. Allee does not suggest this, not because he seeks to maintain a separation between human and non-human communities, but because he cannot say anything more about *this* particular community other than what Darwin had proposed, precisely because he refuses to resort to generalities by switching casually from a given community to a notional community which will serve as an example. I should point out that Allee has no qualms in focusing on both human and non-human communities and groupings between different species, but he is careful always to make such thinking *a starting point*, in such a way that whatever applies to a specific assemblage of living creatures teaches us only what is possible for that group and not what is universally applicable. So, in his writing, following on from descriptions of communities of bees, of quails or of hoofed animals, we come across the somewhat surprising example of the Mennonite communities in North America. These are the Amish people, members of whose Central Committee Allee spoke to in person.[9] In the early decades of the community's existence, when travel was difficult and communication with other colonies limited, the Amish communities could not hope to secure a viable future with fewer than fifty families. Fifty families ensured the relative autonomy of the community because they could support the basic community services: shoe shops, general stores and barbershops, as well as the church and the school, could all be provided by the members of the community and marriages could take place internally. In conditions which were particularly favourable for the pioneers, forty families could just about hope to keep the community going, but below this level the group would be more vulnerable. Marriages would either need to be endogamous or to involve people from outside the community, and increased contacts with the outside world led to ever more disruption as the numbers decreased. But there was also a maximum population size, and above a certain number their system of congregational organization and lay ministry no longer functioned effectively and intra-colonial rivalries often ended up leading to divisions within the community itself. Under the conditions of the time (Allee was writing in the 1940s), the opportunities for travel and improved communications made it possible for communities of between twenty and twenty-five families to survive, provided they could maintain close contacts with others. Below this number, communities remained vulnerable.

The Amish communities were mentioned here not in order to provide a solution to a general problem but to show that each community, no matter how different they might be, faces a specific problem in terms of numbers and of relationships of interdependence. And if Allee turns his attention to the Amish, it is because they have already confronted the problem and have a clear idea of exactly what matters for them and what conditions need to be in place in order to achieve that. These are not therefore 'one size fits all' analogies which eradicate any differences, nor is it a matter of finding the formula or the equation which applies across the board; rather, it is a case of investigating how the same problem can affect any group *bound together* as an aggregation at a given moment of its history – how many do we need to be in order to stay as we are? How many do we need to be to ensure that what matters to us survives? And how, on each occasion, is this problem resolved in a way which is local and appropriate to its time? We can understand, Allee continues, that if under-population is just as much of a problem as overpopulation, and perhaps an even more significant one, certain species turn out to be doomed once they reach a minimum threshold. This is a fact known to those who set themselves the task of eradicating any so-called harmful insects: there is no need to kill all of them since, below a certain threshold, individuals die of natural causes. This is indeed what happened in the case of the much lamented passenger pigeon, a species of bird so prolific that, given their numbers and their apparent enthusiasm to multiply, no one would have regarded them as in any sense fragile. In the case of certain animals there is a threshold below which they are no longer able to reproduce. For many birds, though not all, the presence of others has a beneficial effect up to a certain ceiling, in that it stimulates for example the reproductive functions, even to the extent of synchronizing birds' breeding patterns. In the case of some animals, Allee also points out, their very high visibility means that the effects of low population density can be harmless, whereas in others, such as the muskrat in sparsely populated zones, animals are scattered over a wide area and females, who have a very short period of receptivity, would have little chance of encountering a male. Other animals clearly have more adaptable tolerance thresholds. It is said, for example, that a single couple of Norwegian rats successfully colonized Deget Island in Denmark and that just one couple of reintroduced beavers can give birth to an entire beaver colony. While we cannot force connections between one community and another, we can simply point out that certain problems, though not all, are shared and that certain solutions can be similar, though in each case they are formulated in a different way.

Allee's model, according to which the life of each community can be depicted by a curve which indicates the population thresholds between which the group can survive, did not attract very much interest. According to Judy Stamps, the reasons for this are simple:

researchers who attempted to verify how this curve would look in the populations they were studying observed that minuscule changes in density sometimes produced highly significant and very variable effects on the way animals spread themselves across a particular habitat. Allee's model was therefore abandoned, not, as Stamp makes clear, because it was not realistic, but because researchers did not know how to apply it.[10] In other words, scientists had wanted the model to simplify their lives, but it ended up seriously complicating matters. However, according to Stamps, a number of elements supported Allee's hypothesis – but on condition that certain habits of thought be abandoned, and in particular with reference to the way in which resources were defined. Take the case of females, for example, often considered by researchers simply as resources for males. Except of course that the females themselves would disagree, since they have their own say in the matter and actively choose habitats, territories and males. And if we take this characteristic seriously, it is clear that the success of males will not necessarily decline as a result of their own density within a particular area, and that the contrary is more likely to occur given that the presence of a significant number of males could prove to attract even more females and therefore represent a success criterion. And that would explain why certain birds (and certain hoofed animals) choose, as their territories, display or mating grounds which are always very close to each other.

Clearly the above elements also demonstrate what the population control theory forced us to neglect: the fact that territories are the site of far more complex social activities than these models could allow us to envisage, activities where the art of distance could also, as we shall see, be the art of finding an arrangement with others, of being attuned to them. And undoubtedly this negligence also indicates stubborn habits of thinking which shape the way in which territory is perceived: the obsessive attachment to the idea that territories divide space between 'the haves' and 'the have nots', surreptitiously linking, sometimes even in contradiction to declared intentions, territory and ownership; the fascination with aggressivity – even to the extent of attributing to evolution the praiseworthy effort of having succeeded in channelling it – and, as a corollary, this almost universally held idea that territory favours the strongest and, as a result, prudently ensures the transmission of the best genes.

Counterpoint

Our species has perhaps destroyed its 'own' environment all the more thoroughly because it was not really its own at all.

Fabienne Raphoz, *Parce que l'oiseau*[1]

Of all the theories purporting to explain the purpose of territory, the theory of population control is undoubtedly the one which has ended up carrying the most weight, the one towards which biology, politics or morality have continued to show signs of complicity. From a theoretical point of view, it is also the moment when I felt we had come closest to the concept of territory as property. There is indeed little doubt that its ambition to represent a general organizational theory which would apply equally to all species is not entirely unconnected to this impression. And undoubtedly, too, the theory carries within it the legacy of too many things, of too many assumptions. But, and by no means coincidentally, this theory has also inspired the most barbarous and violent practices I have encountered in the course of this research on territories. In short, such practices set out to establish what would happen if the birds were not there. And, in order to find out, birds were killed.

It is of course true that such methods have also been used to verify other hypotheses. So, to cite just one example, in 1802, at an early stage in ornithological history, the British naturalist George Montagu wrote that male birds sing in order to make themselves visible to females. And, as proof of this, once couples have mated, the singing declines. But this was not sufficient proof for Montagu, and he carried out further experiments to demonstrate that, if the female was taken away, the singing began again.[2] In 1932, the ornithologist Rud Zimmerman killed a number of shrikes who were living as pairs – three males and four females – in order to assess how long it would take for the absent partner to be replaced. These are not unique cases. But with the theory of population control they would become more prevalent.

If, as this theory claims, there are at any one time a number of birds who have not succeeded in finding a mate because they have failed to secure a territory, there must therefore be a supply of single males waiting for their chance to move in. In 1949, the ornithologists Robert Stewart and John Aldrich conducted a study of birds in a section of forest in Maine.[3] They describe how, in association with another research project, they were able to gather a significant amount of information about the population dynamics of birds in a forest near Lake Cross, in the north of the state. The other research project they refer to was a study to determine the effect birds had in controlling numbers of eastern spruce budworms, which the birds feed on. The researchers fail to mention something I discovered for myself, notably that this research was in fact sponsored and financed by the industry which controls timber production in the forests in northern Maine.[4] I will spare readers the details and concentrate on the broader picture. Stewart and Aldrich planned to kill *all* birds within a given area, the so-called experimental area, during the reproductive period, leaving another area of similar size (the control area) intact. The massacre took on apocalyptic proportions, as each time a male bird was killed another came along to replace him. Taking into account all the species concerned, more than twice the number of males present in the first census ended up being destroyed.

I am referring uniquely to male birds here, not because the authors set out to spare the females but because, since these are generally less conspicuous, many of them managed to escape capture, with the exception of those who were nesting and who were therefore easier to locate. Furthermore, Aldrich and Stewart assumed that, once their male had been killed, the females would leave the territory. The rhythm at which replacement occurred, different for each species, allowed the authors to estimate the likely surplus of floaters – that is to say, the likely number of birds waiting for a territory. As a result, the theory concerning the role of territory in population control found itself awarded empirical confirmation. I should add that the following year, in 1950, another team of researchers from Cornell University's conservation institute carried out exactly the same procedure, in the very same location.[5] On that occasion an even greater number of male birds were killed, since the replacement rate was even higher. As the operation took place at a time when laying was well under way, after a particularly mild month of May, many females were also victims of the research project. These experiments therefore confirm Moffat's early theories, and in particular the one claiming that a considerable number of surplus males can be found to be waiting for a territory to be liberated in order to embark on the adventure of reproduction. Moffat also stated that this large population of males without a territory acted as a 'buffer' in cases of very high mortality, since they represented a reserve which enables the species to survive. But, as the authors point out, in the event of repeated catastrophic circumstances, it is impossible to know if this effect would still apply and if the reserve would be substantial enough. And, according to them, and this sends shivers down the spine, only a longer-term study could assess this eventuality.

A few years later, the American ornithologist Gordon Orians would subject red-winged blackbirds and tricoloured blackbirds, both belonging to the passerine family, to a similar treatment in order to support this same theory claiming that territory controls population density.[6] He killed resident males in order to ascertain how quickly their territory was reoccupied. In the early 1970s, the Scottish ornithologists Adam Watson and Robert Moss subjected red grouse to a similar investigation. Taking as their starting point the observation that, in certain years, the population was extremely dense and territories were greatly reduced in extent, they wondered why there were so many grouse in some areas and not in others. They fertilized the soil so as to assess the influence of the quality of food supplies on reproduction, injected males with testosterone in order to measure the effects of aggression on territory size, and destroyed some birds so as to measure how quickly they would be replaced.[7]

With a general theory of an optimal balance which would be imposed everywhere and for all, we are a very long way from theories which describe an efflorescence of fragile local environments, with all the adjustments and delicate relationships these might entail. A long way too from the various inventions and experiments which in the end affirm what Shirley Strum, the American primatologist and baboon specialist, endearingly refers to as the tolerance of natural selection to trials and errors. Above all, we are a long way from the modes of attention by means of which certain scientists strive to ensure they are sensitive to what they are observing, or simply become so by seeking to understand what matters to their birds. Such as, for example, the use of such practices as banding in order to monitor and recognize birds, a practice Margaret Nice is confident does not trouble them. These are attachment practices – banding or ringing a bird, by a fortuitous coincidence, means creating an alliance, a form of engagement, with it.[8] But it is an asymmetric engagement from which nothing is expected of the bird itself. Instead, from that moment onwards, it is the researcher herself who is committed. Or, similarly, the case of Jared Verner who, touched by the clumsiness of Male number 25, the long-billed marsh wren who had until that point been beset by misfortunes, made sure the nest was fastened securely to prevent it from falling down.

I cannot of course guarantee that the theory of population control which lay behind such practices inspired or facilitated them. It might very well be pointed out that such methods were not unusual at that time. Certainly, a great many experiments destined to establish in what way the presence of a living creature matters have failed to find any simpler way of doing so than by substituting presence with absence – a method which features in scientific literature under the watered-down name of 'bird collections'. And it could also be pointed out that the accusation I am levelling towards these researchers is that of a particular period, our own, in which it is no longer possible to ignore the fact that birds might at some point no longer exist. But the issue of extinction is not the only one that matters here. Living in a damaged world has modified our emotional responses, and it is from this perspective that I reinterpret such situations. These emotional responses, or affects, correspond to what Baptiste Morizot so aptly calls 'solastalgia', the feeling of having lost the solace of a familiar world, and the awareness of the loss and of what it is we are losing.[9] And it is from this perspective, no doubt somewhat unjustly, that I find myself thinking of these devastated and wasted lives (an aspect that ends up being somewhat masked by the problem of the extinction of a species but about which this story makes us so aware),[10] of the fear and the sense of terror that those birds must have felt when their familiar environment suddenly ceased to make sense, those hunted males, those females driven out of their nests, the newcomers caught in a trap which they were unable to understand. It is with such feelings of loss, of anger and of sadness that I judge a world and its practices, a world not so very old, but one permeated with affects and emotions which no longer make sense to me. But I can also turn to other practices that were happening at the same time as these 'collections' and which refused to follow in their footsteps, practices which were attentive, which took care of those they were observing, and which involved researchers ready to respond to the interest that birds had aroused in them.

It will be recalled that Allee described those conducting experiments as 'impatient', since nature never responded to their questions quickly enough. Allee was no doubt right in his view, but I think that this theory involves more than mere impatience, even though it shares with it the characteristic of authorizing, promoting even, certain forms of inattention. I believe that the very existence of the theory of population control, the theoretical gesture itself, informs and shapes how scientists engage with their subject of investigation. These are 'careless' theories, poorly attached to the focus of their inquiry, and which end up being forcibly imposed. Once again, a case of everything moving too fast and without sufficient thought.

Nor, in the case of those birds caught up in the problem posed by the caterpillars, can I claim with any certainty which of the two projects was behind this methodology – the one aimed at verifying the population control theory or the one which financed the research, and which consisted in evaluating the effect of predation on the caterpillars by simplifying their ecosystem to an extreme. But, in each of these two cases, there is clearly a common dimension to be found in the motives behind the research. Such practices, whether motivated by an economic (or Malthusian) theory of how exploitation of resources is managed, or whether ostensibly working for the cause of industries exploiting the forests, have both inherited the same modern conception of nature which contaminates them: the idea that the environment is above all else, and perhaps exclusively, a resource to be exploited. Something to be appropriated and which we are at liberty to use and abuse as we wish.[11]

SECOND CHORD

Counterpoint

A territory borrows from all the milieus;
it bites into them, seizes them bodily (although
it remains vulnerable to intrusions).

Gilles Deleuze and Félix Guattari[1]

'Territory, my friend Marcos Matteo Diaz tells me, calls for a territorial approach. And a true territorial approach involves finding some leeway within the territory.' And he adds: 'Then you can breathe freely again.'[2] When he made those remarks, I still had not fully realized just how right he was. A territory is a place where all sorts of things and events are played out again in a different way – where ways of doing things, ways of being, are opened up to other connections, to other assemblages. Thinking about territory therefore calls for certain particular gestures: it means trying to create some leeway when consequences adhere too closely to causes, when functions tie behaviours too firmly to selective pressures, when ways of being are reduced so as to obey a handful of principles. And that also means slowing down the pace, letting some fresh air in, giving free rein to the imagination. It means stepping out of the territory and then re-entering it. It was on rereading *A Thousand Plateaux* by Gilles Deleuze and Félix Guattari that I understood what Marcos meant.

I had to reread it. I might as well confess from the start that, initially, I had some difficulties with Deleuze. I regarded him with a certain amount of irritated suspicion and disliked the way he referred to animals. It may be something of a digression, but I was disturbed by the fact that he poured scorn on pets and judged those who loved them so harshly, whether in the interviews in *From A to Z*,[3] under the letter 'A for animal', or in the book *A Thousand Plateaux*. In this book, Deleuze and Guattari have no qualms about treating those who become attached to their dog or cat as 'fools' and in being scathing about elderly women.[4] In her book *When Species Meet*, Donna Haraway reproached them on the subject in no uncertain terms,[5] asking whether Deleuze and Guattari are not in fact displaying a deep scorn for the everyday, for the ordinary. Did they not display a total lack of curiosity towards real animals – even though these are often invoked within their work? I was completely on her side. For me, it felt as if the animals were being used as hostages in a problem that did not concern them. And this was certainly true as far as pets were concerned. But, in the interests of honesty, I should add that the issue is not so much about pets as about animals which have been *made into* 'familial' pets: the ones who are thought of only in terms of filiation in relation to human roles, indeed to the relationships underlying the oedipal familial structures – the father, the grandfather, the mother, the little brother – the authors referring specifically here to the language of psychoanalysis. It is not therefore relationships in general with pets which meet with their disapproval but rather *human* relationships with them. People who truly love animals, they say, have an animal relationship with animals. Certainly, but I am still not totally convinced and I am not sure I want to be. The problem with taking hostages is that it is always problematic to claim, on behalf of the hostages, '*Not in my name!*'

End of parenthesis. Territories are what interests me right now. And territories constitute one of the most fundamental and crucial concepts in *A Thousand Plateaux*, and in particular in chapter 11 ('Of the Refrain'). I had read it at the beginning of my research and, I have to admit, there too, I found it difficult. On the one hand, it all seemed too abstract, too unconnected with what I was looking for; or, perhaps more to the point, none of it seemed to help me establish exactly what it was I was looking for. Moreover, it rekindled the same feeling of irritation I had felt on reading their judgement on pets: that sense of things moving too quickly, the same sense of disappointment and of uneasiness that I had experienced with Serres and his *Malfeasance*. Let me emphasize that this was uneasiness, since I can only agree with Serres, with his anger and with what he was trying to make us feel. And I could have been wholeheartedly in agreement with his desire to render the pollution of our environment *intolerable* to us. But not at that price, not in that way. I experienced the same sense of uneasiness with Deleuze and Guattari, in spite of the enormous difference in their respective approach, because there again it seemed to me that everything was going too fast, that not enough attention was being focused on potential differences – I think that essentially the very mention of 'animals' unsettles me.

That sense of uneasiness was all the more acute in that *A Thousand Plateaux* is essentially a machine designed to create concepts, a difficult book which is intimidating, though without constituting what Deleuze, referring to philosophy, calls 'a formidable school of intimidation',[6] a school designed to prevent thinking.

On the contrary in fact, from start to finish, this book sets out to make us think. And it was precisely for that reason that I needed to learn how to read it, letting myself be guided not by the words but by its gestures, its rhythms, its pauses, by its stammering, its spluttering, its emotions.[7] I needed to abandon my customary way of approaching the reading of scientific articles, which consisted in gleaning information, identifying facts and knowledge. I had almost forgotten that the task of philosophy is not to inform but, instead, to slow down, to slip *out of tune*, to hesitate. To slip out of tune in order to find other ways of being in tune. To seek a change of direction when the road ahead is too straight. To be caught up by different forces. To give facts a power that we do not ourselves possess and that we will need to learn to construct alongside them, that of *making things happen*, of producing effects and unexpected effects. What I am describing here are movements, and this is what I was trying to learn from Deleuze and Guattari, even if the movements I describe are not always faithful to theirs. It is a matter of understanding them in my own way[8] (not simply referring to them, therefore, but engaging with them)[9] – or, in other words, finally hearing what it was they were striving to make us hear: not interpreting, but experiencing.

And that is exactly what they were proposing by bringing territory into their work. If the word appears at a very early stage in *A Thousand Plateaux* (on page 9 of the text), it refers at this point not to animals but to the task of writing which Deleuze and Guattari have imposed on themselves: 'Write, form a rhizome, increase your territory by deterritorialization . . .'[10] It is clear from the outset that the territory to which they refer takes on its full sense only in relation to this other term, this concept they have created, which is that of 'deterritorialization'. It is therefore no coincidence that this term appears even earlier in the book, on the third page. 'A book', they write, 'exists only through the outside and on the outside', through its connections with other assemblages, other multiplicities into which its own multiplicity is inserted and metamorphosed. The meaning of 'deterritorialize', and the significance of this term, begins to be clear: deterritorializing means undoing an existing assemblage – but in order to reterritorialize within another one. It means undoing one way of being territorialized by connecting to other assemblages and reterritorializing through them. Territorializing therefore means entering into an assemblage which territorializes whatever becomes part of it. And this means that any territorialization involves, first of all, a process where something is deterritorialized in order to be reterritorialized in a different form. Consequently, therefore, whether in the context of writing or with reference to birds, we should refer not so much to territories as to *acts of territorialization*.

It is in this sense that all the various actions carried out by animals in the process of becoming territorial begin to make sense. The refrain (the endless repetition of rhythms), the markings, the colours, the displays and, especially in the case of birds, the songs: 'The territory is in fact an act that affects milieus and rhythms, that "territorializes" them. The territory is the product of a territorialization of milieus and rhythms. It amounts to the same thing to ask when milieus and rhythms become territorialized and what the difference is between a non-territorial animal and a territorial animal.'[11]

Acts, milieus and rhythms: the territory appeared to us first as a spatial configuration, identifiable because installed in a relatively enduring manner in space. On reading Deleuze and Guattari, I begin to realize that there is in fact nothing more '*dynamic*' than a territory, no matter how stable its borders might be or how faithful to it the residents may be. First of all – but we are already aware of this, because territory is not so much about space as about distances – territorialization is the literal and expressive act (in other words, the performance) of 'marking one's distance'. Distance is not a measure but an intensity, a rhythm. Territory is always in a rhythmic relationship to something else. Next, because territorialization represents a process of metamorphosis. But this metamorphosis is not the simple metamorphosis of a creature whose whole life is drastically changed. It affects each of the functions involved in the process of becoming territorial (such as the aggressive function, for example), it 'changes pace', it reorganizes. Aggression is 'deterritorialized' of its functions in order to be reterritorialized on the territory (which means effectively that it is territorialized). And, consequently, it no longer bears any relationship to aggressivity, except in respect to the form it takes: it has become expressive, pure form. Property, in this sense, and Souriau asserts this along with Deleuze and Guattari, is permeated with artistic intentions.

The territorialized being is not only another way of being but a way of being for which everything becomes matters of expression. More precisely: 'There is a territory precisely when milieu components cease to be directional, becoming dimensional instead, when they cease to be functional to become expressive. There is a territory when the rhythm has expressiveness. What defines the territory is the emergence of matters of expression (qualities).'[12] As we shall see, contrary to what Konrad Lorenz assumed, territory is not the result of aggressivity, nor does it control it.

The shift in approach proposed by Deleuze and Guattari is important. Territory is a place where everything becomes rhythm, melodic landscape, motifs and counterpoints, matters of expression. Territory is the result of art. Territory creates and therefore insists that our thinking be guided by new relationships.

> Expressiveness is not reducible to the immediate effects of an impulse triggering an action in a milieu: ... *expressive qualities or matters of expression enter shifting relations with one another that 'express' the relation of the territory they draw to the interior milieu of impulses and exterior milieu of circumstances.* To express is not to depend upon; there is an autonomy of expression.[13]

The interior impulses are no longer just simple causes but the melodic counterpoints of external circumstances.

As a result, each of the functions which have been territorialized, transformed in an expressive process, can take on an autonomy and end up becoming part of another assemblage, another functional organization. This would explain, for example, how, in certain birds, sexuality, which is another form of assemblage even when it appears as a territorialized function, can sometimes be independent from it, keeping 'its distance' from it, or how the most diverse forms of sociality are created in which the territory is fully implicated. So, for example, when another bird of the same species is greeted without aggressivity, it could be said that the territorial assemblage opens onto 'a social assemblage that has gained autonomy', the partner therefore becoming "'an animal with home value"'.[14] Or, as certain ornithologists have suggested, the song that the male offers to the female, in the course of mating rituals, can represent a reappropriation of the territorial song that the male had sung to other males ... There is indeed nothing more dynamic than a territory. And nothing would be sadder than a failure to perceive it as part of a regime of emergences, of beauty, of counterpoints and of inventions. And of movements out of the territory.

It was clear that, in order to overcome my difficulties, I would need to abandon the idea of understanding *everything* and simply allow myself to be permeated by the ideas. And it was equally clear that, once I had done my research in the various scientific articles, I would need to have access to a body of facts, of stories, of theories, which would provide me with a benchmark against which to measure their proposals in the context of a reality made up of events, of animals, of acts, of behaviours, of functions, and enable me to feel, in rereading their words, no longer a sense that I was dealing with abstractions but, instead, an ever growing familiarity with what they are proposing.

I would need carefully to preserve everything I had learned about birds, and, just as carefully, treasure the multiplicity of worlds which were emerging thanks to ornithologists. Hold on to the fact that some of these are not simply seeking to formulate different *theories* about territory but instead to observe and record the multiple different ways of territorializing. And be aware that, on the one hand, the quest to identify the functions of territory and, on the other, the challenge scientists face in recognizing that both the apparent meaningless-ness and the endless inventiveness of bird behaviour exert a powerful constraint. And sometimes severely impede their movements. What Deleuze and Guattari offered me was the opportunity to learn how to follow potential deterritorializations, to leave territories in order to re-enter them in a better way, to make them 'bite into' all milieus. To learn how to deterritorialize territories as they were portrayed in all these stories, in all these articles and scientific reports, in order to reterritorialize them in other assemblages. In the same way that so many different behaviours, so many sentiments, so many inherited structures have the capacity to be replayed in the adventure of life, reconfiguring and taking on new forms – an embryonic feather can provide warmth, then be part of a courtship display and finally, a very long time later, evolve into flight; a song can indicate possession, mark out distances, give rhythm to a territory and then be deterritorialized and become instead a call to draw attention, to raise the alarm or to attract a mate – the stories that I had collected would need to link to other stories, to be open to other experiments, to 'change pace' themselves. They would be part of a genuine territorial approach – one that would bring in a gust of 'backyard air' in the words of Bob Dylan, aptly cited by Deleuze.[15] In other words, the chance to breathe freely again . . .

4

Possessions

In an extract cited by Margaret Nice, Howard wrote as follows: 'a more varied or a less precarious food supply, a sparse population, or a serviceable pair of wings may all bring emancipation from a system which is undoubtedly a strain and an oppression to the birds that are forced to live under it.' In response to this assertion, Nice made it clear that she could not agree with this idea that birds were subjected to oppression by being forced to live under such a system. Her observations of song sparrows had enabled her to see that the permanent residents remained on the same territory all through the winter, a territory they were 'unwilling to leave or defend'.[1]

I believe that this difference of opinion draws attention to an important question. First of all, it is often said that a map cannot represent a territory. Nor does territory correspond to a specific space. As we have seen, the same space, the inhabited space, can be a territory at certain times and not at others. Territory imposes a rhythm on space. It is possible to be a permanent resident, like the song sparrow, and not be territorial during the winter, although, as Nice demonstrates, still continuing to live in the same place. The theory advanced by Nice implies moreover that territory is a matter of desire, or rather of many different desires – the desire to defend it in the spring, the desire simply to remain there throughout the winter. Space is, I would suggest, a matter of variable affectivity.

But the situation is more complex than that, and the notion of space that I am using here cannot fully explain this 'variable affectivity'. I shall attempt to complicate matters. The Swiss biologist Heini Hediger also looked at the problem of space from the perspective of freedom: 'the free animal does not live in freedom: neither in space nor as regards its behaviour towards other animals.'[2] They do not live in freedom because they are only familiar with a minuscule segment of the potential space – I should, however, point out that Hediger worked for many years with animals in captivity in his role as director of zoos in Basel, Berne and Zurich, and we may indeed wonder whether he is not simply repeating a well-worn argument. But if we set aside, for the moment, the notion of freedom as he sees it, what he has to say is certainly interesting. Hediger explains that an individual animal's living space, far from being homogeneous, is in fact highly differentiated. Animals often become attached to certain places and completely ignore others, as though – and here Hediger borrows a metaphor from the German biologist and philosopher Jakob von Uexküll – the animals' tracks correspond to a thread of highly fluid medium within a viscous mass – rhythms of the density of a milieu. It is rare for animals to be unaware of the somewhat strict limits of their space. Admittedly, Hediger points out, birds of prey or snakes, as well as some species artificially transplanted by humans, such as the brown rat, the house mouse or the common sparrow, have become, to use his term,[3] 'cosmopolitan'.

We must not imagine, however, that these cosmopolitans 'enjoy the run' of their enormous territory in the sense that they travel from end to end of it. The development of so many local varieties that the systematist finds himself in serious difficulties points to the fact that even these animals tend to keep to definite limits within their main range.

And further on he adds that birds should be thought of as 'living creatures linked to particular localities'.

The territorial space is therefore a space which has a double role in that it both affects and assigns,[4] so that a given space is *assigned* for territorialization and at the same time is *affected* by territorialization. Yet the notion of space still remains too narrow. Remember the example given by Lorenz about cats making use of the same site but at different times. In this case, territory is not so much a geographical space as a space governed by the rhythm of time. Space, in other words, is defined by both time and usage and derives its qualities from both of these. Other dimensions and other aspects relating to usage can also affect it. The tricoloured blackbirds observed by Gordon Orians live in territories where the dense vegetation forms a sort of low-growing canopy, made up of reed-like plants called cattails. The bird does perform an aerial display but asserts his territorial presence on a low platform formed from bent-over cattails. Everything above the vegetation remains unterritorialized – for blackbirds the sky belongs to all birds. It is a neutral space in which males and females can go about their business and are free to explore without being threatened. But if a male, identified as an intruder, ventures beneath the vegetation, he will be immediately attacked. The territory encodes everything: the same bird, depending on whether he is under the shelter of the cattail canopy or in the sky, can be either an 'intruder' or 'simply a passing conspecific'; he can be 'territorialized' and 'deterritorialized' according to the space he is passing through. And the same is true in the case of the red-eyed vireo, a small passerine found in forests in North America. These birds mark out their space in the shape of a narrow cylinder about 25 metres high which extends from about ground level up to the height of the leaf canopy. The yellow-throated vireo lives in the same areas, but its territory extends over a wide area and involves only the high parts of the canopy.

If territory extends into space, this space does not bear much resemblance to what we, who are attached to the earth, call 'surface area'. In reality, it is probably an effect of stratifications which, except in a few rare cases, we are unable to detect. A multi-layered 'mille-feuille' of different usages. But that is not all.

In an article published in the magazine *British Birds* in 1934, the British ornithologist Julian Huxley describes an astonishing phenomenon.[5] It is worth pointing out that, in the article, he notes that what he observed took place during a visit of a few days to Henry Eliot Howard in Hartlebury, Worcestershire, at the very end of December 1933. Huxley arrived on 30 December, and the two men observed birds together over the following few days. If I mention this here, it is not because this kind of detail is altogether unexpected, given that *British Birds* is a monthly publication read by amateur ornithologists rather than a true scientific review and therefore does not necessarily insist on the same conventions as academic literature. This distinction certainly allowed Huxley to include in the article observations made by Howard after his departure as well as some made before he arrived. It is essentially a kind of joint signature, a reappropriation of work by one of the two participants. This detail probably also serves to indicate the bonds of friendship between the two researchers, and the fact that it was New Year's Eve the day after Huxley's arrival was no coincidence. I could not help being touched and intrigued by this information. It is evidence that birds inspire social bonds between humans – and this is by no means unusual, as we discover in reading certain biographies where we learn that many researchers were in the habit of visiting colleagues in their places of work, often staying with them for several days. But I also want to emphasize the fact that Huxley's work, on the subject of what 'home' might mean for animals, was conducted in what was his colleague's home – a melodic counterpoint in my territorialized imagination which finds itself drawn to questions of hospitality. I can almost hear the invitation to 'make yourself at home'; I can practically feel the warmth of the guest room, the eiderdowns, the whiskey and the wood fires. And no doubt research on territory is steeped in this 'homely' dimension which extends well beyond the simple matter of hospitality offered to researchers visiting their colleagues. Indeed, a considerable amount of research on territory (not all of it, but a significant amount nonetheless) could be carried out 'at home', in the form of 'home-based' science, and this helps to explain the large number of amateurs, of 'ornithophiles' as Fabienne Raphoz calls them,[6] who would eventually become professional ornithologists. It might also explain why certain women were able to combine research and family life (Margaret Nice in her garden and in the area adjoining her home in Columbus, Barbara Blanchard on the campus at Berkeley, home to the two groups of white-crowned sparrows she compared).

Returning to our story, on 31 December Huxley and Howard visited an artificial pond which was home to a number of common coots. Several couples had established territories there, and it was evident from observation of their behaviour that the space had indeed been divided up into a number of different territories. During the night of 31 December to 1 January there was a heavy frost. On returning to the pond on his own, Huxley noticed that much of the water surface had frozen over. Among all the birds visible at that moment, only one couple, the ones occupying the part of the pond which had remained unfrozen, were still displaying territorial behaviour. The other birds, Huxley recounts, whose territories had frozen over, appeared to have abandoned their territorial instinct.

Even more astonishingly, he noted that, if a neighbouring male bird ventured onto the territory of the couple who were still demonstrating territorial behaviour, the male did not react as long as the other bird remained on the frozen area. The ice, Huxley concluded, had in a sense transformed the territory into 'neutral ground'. The other members of the group, deterritorialized by the ice, occasionally grouped together and appeared to occupy the space in a relatively indifferent manner, with the exception of the section defended by the couple still exhibiting territorial behaviour. It must be inferred, Huxley concluded, that territorial behaviour depends not only on an internal physiological state but also on the external state of the terrain, its actual presence.

Clearly the properties of space are capable of change. And, if we refer to territorial behaviour, we should no doubt assume that the milieu or environment itself also 'behaves', that it *allows itself*, or refuses, *to be appropriated*. Space co-opts modes of attention, ways of being. According to Thibault De Meyer, the philosopher and specialist in ethology, it contains forces, powers, which acts of territorialization seek out. And not all spaces turn out to be suitable or appropriate.[7] If territorial behaviour is a behaviour of appropriation, it is not in the most common sense of 'possessing' or of acquiring but in the sense of adapting something, making it your 'own'. But I am perhaps going too fast here. Let us go back to Nice and her song sparrows. In winter, the sparrows live in a space which for us, from a spatial point of view, is the same as the one they occupy during the summer. But, in the spring or summer, this space is no longer *the same for the birds who themselves are not the same*: they have, for that period of time, become territorial, something therefore not intrinsic to them but, rather, a way of being, or, in other words, a way of living, which metamorphoses them. Or, rather, a way of living which

metamorphoses the assemblage of the bird and the space within time.
Something has happened. Territory is therefore not a spatial issue
but rather something which is played out according to a system of
intensities and temporality – that is to say, according to a rhythm. It
is, to return to von Uexküll, a lived space, but more particularly one
which is *lived in an intense way* – in other words, one permeated by
different intensities.

When I say that the properties of a space are capable of change,
it is first of all to indicate that space can be experienced in different ways, that, as in the case of the coots observed by Howard and
Huxley, it can be at one moment part of a territorial configuration
and at another, quite *literally*, be deterritorialized. But who or what
is deterritorialized? The frozen area of the lake or the coot who no
longer experiences the territory as his own? I would say both of
these, precisely because both have been disappropriated, after having
been appropriated to each other. Through the process of territorialization, space has become part of a system of appropriation. Which
does not imply that it is the *object* of appropriation. Here I use the
word 'appropriation' not in the sense attributed to it by Serres but
according to the definition used by Souriau, a sense which brings
together both the specific particularities of something and the notion
of that if something is appropriated it is made appropriate. As David
Lapoujade writes, for Souriau,

> possession doesn't entail the appropriation of a good or a being.
> Appropriation isn't concerned with property (*la propriété*) but with par-
> ticularities (*le propre*). When we speak of appropriation, we shouldn't
> use the verb's pronominal voice but its active voice: to possess isn't to
> appropriate (*s'approprier*) but to adapt to . . . (*approprier à . . .*) – in other
> words, to make something exist in its own right (*en propre*).

Or, put another way, and this will make things even clearer, we could say that the being in question appropriates, or adapts, his or her existence to new dimensions.[8] We find a very similar idea in the work of the jurist Sarah Vanuxem, when she turns to French legal history and anthropology for interpretations which will make it possible to dispense with the conception of property as a sovereign right over objects in order to think of things as *milieus* which can be lived in: 'In the mountain "douars" of the Shilha people, to appropriate a place consists in both shaping it to yourself and shaping yourself to it; appropriating land is to attribute it to yourself and to give yourself over to it.'[9] In other words, we are territorialized just as much as we territorialize.

Let us return to the as yet unresolved question of freedom, which will enable us to explore this argument further. Provided, that is, that we reformulate it differently. It is not helpful to insist here on the fact, referred to earlier, that, in another section of his book, the same Howard asserted that territory gave birds freedom because, as a meeting ground, it allowed them to come and go at will, confident that they would always be able to meet up there. This is not what is at issue here. In referring to 'oppression' in the citation above, Howard emphasizes the fact that the territory in a sense imposes an 'obligation' on birds. Howard interprets this obligation, in his own particular theoretical context, in terms of determinisms, or functions – the territory has a 'hold' on the bird because of food supply, a 'hold' because of the risk of overpopulation, a 'hold' because of the bird's inability to go elsewhere. But if the territory exerts a hold in so many different ways, not to mention the numerous functions previously listed by Howard, can we not simply conclude that the territory *exerts a hold* over the bird? What Howard is describing when he refers to this sense of oppression (and he is probably right, except that this oppression is the territory itself, not what it is used for, however indisputable that may be) might surely be the fact that, when a bird inhabits a territory, he or she is completely inhabited by that territory. The term 'possession', which it has been preferable to avoid until now, takes on its full meaning: the bird possesses its territory, because it is itself possessed by that territory. It has adapted its existence to the new dimensions offered by the territory; it has been caught up in a process of territorialization. It is the territory which makes the bird sing, just as it is also the territory which makes it fly to and fro, dance, display its colours. In other words, the bird has become territorial, which means that its whole being has been territorialized. Possession, in this case, refers just as much to possessing as to being possessed.

I mentioned earlier, in reference to the Rocky Mountains goats and what Hediger said about certain animals, that territorial marking is also a form of extending the body of the animal, a territorial mammal in that instance, in space. In this context, I observed that acts of territorialism were a way of transforming the space not into 'their own' but into 'themselves'. Territorialization reconfigures what initially constitutes the notion of 'self' and 'non-self', all the more so given that certain mammals 'mark' themselves with the scents of their territory – earth, humus, carrion, vegetation . . . In doing so they become all the more territorialized in that they *are* the territory. Territory is the expression of a 'self', physically and literally, and the 'self' becomes the expression of the territory. Yes, people will say to me, but birds rarely 'mark' in the same way. Birds sing. They never stop singing. The difference between them and mammals is, in this respect, as I have already emphasized, a crucial one: these are very different modes of presence.

But what Deleuze and Guattari propose in their book leads me to think that, beyond this difference, there is a deep-seated similarity of purpose. Birds sing. Have you ever travelled by train with head-phones on? Have you felt, as has often been my own experience, that the passing landscape could be 'Bach-like' or 'Tchaikovsky-like', or sensed to what extent music imprints itself, covers and affects our surroundings? An accordion in the metro can change not only our mood but even our way of perceiving things. The world becomes not musical but melodic. And rather than being simply a melody associated with a landscape, 'the melody itself is a sonorous landscape'.[10] Put differently, the act of territorialization is, among other things, an act in which a space becomes musicalized – I stress 'among other things', because there are also the displays, the dance rituals, the staged threats, the colours, the beating of wings. And the constant flying to and fro in order to patrol the space.

When observing a bird in the process of setting up its territory, it is impossible not to notice the endless repetitions of these patrol flights (like the songs, everything is based on repetition). We described right at the beginning how the bird chooses a high point, then begins to fly to and fro within a space which gradually, as a result of these repeated comings and goings, these rhythmic patrols, forms the appropriated space. It might be supposed that by means of these 'patrol flights' the bird is, on the one hand, drawing attention to his territory and, on the other, making himself 'at home' by establishing a deep intimacy with a place thus 'appropriated' and with its particularities, a process in which the chosen space becomes 'familiar'. But, by flying to and fro in this way, the bird is also doing something else. He is drawing in invisible ink a dense web stretched above the space gradually filled up by his presence. The song accompanies this activity and is itself a reflection of those flights, creating, as we read in *A Thousand Plateaux*, 'a wall of sound, or at least a wall with some sonic bricks in it'. But it is not so much a wall as an overlapping mosaic (the term 'wall' suggests the notion of limits, and what matters here goes beyond such a concept), or any term which could convey the process of enveloping an area, like spinning a web woven of movements and songs. The song functions to some extent like a spider's web. The web woven by the spider extends the limits of the spider's body in space; it *is* the spider's body, and all the space caught in the web, which becomes the web-space, the body-space, this space which was until then the milieu or the surroundings becomes a property of the spider not in the usual sense, but in the sense that it possesses certain particularities (that is what appropriation means, as Lapoujade reminds us: the fact of making something exist in its own right). From this perspective, Deleuze was right in translating Jacob von Uexküll's *Umwelt* not as 'the world as it is experienced' or as the 'environment' but as the 'associated milieu': for the web, and therefore the space filled by the web, is an associated milieu of the spider's body, an extended body (just as my arm is associated with my body while being at the same time both a part of it and an extension of it).

If the song is an extension of the bird's body, the bird could perhaps be said to be sung by its song, just as the body of the spider becomes the web and forms new relationships with what surrounds it – relationships which could deterritorialize the expressive modality, when the web becomes a trap without, however, ceasing to be a means of expression and of 'impressions'. The bird's song will therefore be expressive power, 'extensive' power, and it is not impossible that the power of this song, its rhythm and its intensity, will to some extent determine the possible extension of what will become territory, in a way similar to that achieved by patrolling an area by continuously flying to and fro. In other words, *the bird's song becomes one with the space*. Quite literally. The song is the expressive mode through which a sung space *takes shape* and becomes the bird's body. In an extract from a novel by Maylis de Kerangal, I found a particularly power-ful description of this relationship between a song in the process of becoming a territory and a territory becoming a song, of this process of 'becoming one' with space through which the bird appropriates its territory, its place, its extended self. In this extract, Kerangal is writ-ing about the goldfinches of Algiers. Describing Hocine, the young man who traps and sells them, she writes:

> He knew every species, its characteristics and metabolism, could tell from the way it sang the provenance of each bird, even the name of the forest where it was born . . . But the appeal of the goldfinch went beyond the musicality of its song and was linked, above all, to geography: its song was the manifestation of a territory. Valley, city, mountain, forest, hill, stream. It brought a landscape to life, evoked a topography, gave the feeling of a soil and a climate. A piece of the planetary puzzle took form in its beak, . . . the goldfinch expectorated something solid, scented, tactile and coloured. So it was that Hocine's eleven birds sang the cartography of a vast territory.[11]

In this way the song of each of these goldfinches incorporates a per-spective on a world – that of Bainem forest, Kaddous, Dély Ibrahim or Souk Ahras. Each of these birds represents the experience of a fragment of a world; it embodies it. The song has marked the terri-tory, the territory has marked the song.

With the help of this perspective, many stories can be reread. They can become part of another assemblage, find new roles in other regimes of possession, acquire a counterpoint – and in doing so their musicality also changes. Take, for example, the case of those females who were said to have chosen a territory and *not* a male. But the 'and not' here is already superfluous, it is no longer possible to be in an 'either . . . or' situation, as though song, courtship display, colours, poses, territorializing acts and territory could somehow be disassociated.

Territory has been seen purely in terms of resources. These are of course important, but are they really what matters most? That would mean first of all forgetting that, in establishing a territory, the bird is creating a space which it fills to the brim with attractions: the highest point, which becomes the central focus of attraction, the boundary as the focus of relations with the outside, and the bird itself, an attractor using patterns, poses, signs and songs. The territory is a device for attracting attention, a trap baited with attractions, whether for other males or for passing females. Secondly, to assume that the female chooses a territory and not a mate, and that she bases her choice on the available resources, means neglecting the fact that she is entering into an alliance with a composition created by the male in relation to a place, a space. What does she feel, what does she see, what does she hear in that composition? How does she sense how successfully, or unsuccessfully, the bird has appropriated himself to that task? How does she know if he has succeeded in appropriating himself to what has now become *his* place? And if the bird's song has become the expression of a place, no doubt she will recognize in its signature the height of the trees, the presence of a neighbourhood, whether peaceful or noisy – as we shall see, that can be important – the rough texture of the rocks, the presence of a spring with a song of its own, the shade canopy, the taste of its fruits or of insects under the leaves, and perhaps even the way the sunlight filters through the foliage. All expressions of intensity, all variations of intensity potentially mapped out in the bird's song. A musicography in fact.

Counterpoint

The Canadian ornithologist Louis Lefebvre conducted an extended comparative study on intelligence in birds. It was a genuine study rather than just a single experiment, in that he set out to collect anecdotes relating to innovative behaviour by exploring sixty-five years of scientific literature and reports written by amateurs, using the key words 'unusual', 'new' or 'first case observed'. The result amounted to 2,300 examples from across hundreds of different species. Most of the anecdotes were about feeding behaviours. This does not entirely surprise me. Feeding is clearly an important element in animal lives, but, as we have already seen, such behaviour also tends to be the one most frequently observed by researchers. Firstly, this is because animals are more visible when they are feeding. While they can successfully conceal many aspects of their behaviour, they are nevertheless constrained by the location of their food supplies. Also, if some behaviours can temporarily be put on hold because animals are disturbed by the presence of an observer, it is harder to delay feeding to some more convenient moment, particularly if the observer is a patient one.[1] Let us return to Lefebvre. Among hundreds of examples, he discovered that an Antarctic brown skua, a predatory sea bird, snuggled in alongside baby seal pups in order to suckle their mother's milk, that a cowbird used a twig to help it pick through cow dung, that green herons use insects as bait by placing them on the water surface in order to attract fish, that a seagull killed a rabbit by dropping it from a height, a technique normally associated with dropping shellfish from high up in order to break them, or that, during the Zimbabwean war of liberation, vultures perched on the barbed wire fences of minefields and waited until gazelles or other herbivores wandered into the trap.

Jennifer Ackerman, who refers to this research in her own book on the intelligent life of birds, speculates as to whether all this amounts to intelligence or to an element of daring, a readiness to experiment.[2] She concludes that, in any case, a willingness to experiment is an advantage when it comes to solving problems. Technical ability, the invention of tools, she says, seems to represent the ultimate success criterion for defining intelligence. On this subject, she cites two researchers, Alex Taylor and Russell Gray, who assert that a list of the tools man has invented 'is a useful proxy for the entire history of our species'. Indeed. But this list of technical advances which 'created revolutions in the societies they were invented in', and which includes pottery, the wheel, paper, fire and clothes, also includes concrete, gunpowder, the automobile and the nuclear bomb. This is serious stuff.

Far be it from me to neglect the role of technical skills or to denigrate the significance of these, both in their own right and in the way they have shaped us. *Homo faber*. But I find myself remembering Ursula Le Guin's essay 'The Carrier Bag Theory of Fiction',[3] that magical revolt against the great sagas of virility, that antidote to the epic poison of victorious man, creator of weapons. In this essay, Le Guin makes the case for other stories and, in particular, stories featuring the invention of the 'container', of the envelope, those precious and fragile objects which enable us to keep, transport, protect, carry something to someone: 'a leaf a gourd a shell a net a bag a sling a sack a bottle a pot a box a container. A holder. A recipient.' The things which keep beings and objects safe.

For my own part, I would want to add other stories to these, stories telling of social inventions, of inventions which were pivotal and as diverse as it is possible to imagine, thanks to which living creatures have learned how to live together, to form a society or to create communities of life. Not in harmony – it would indeed require exceptional circumstances or a great deal of effort to succeed in getting the wolf to lie down with the lamb. At best that would be called domestication and, no matter what the circumstances, would always come at a price.[4] Not in harmony, but something very like it.

As we have seen earlier, territories are no Garden of Eden, and life within them can involve conflicts of interests and often incompatible desires. Yet somehow it all *holds together.* I would like to find stories which celebrate these successes. However, if technology has indeed led to inventions which have shaped us, and if we can congratulate our ancestors for some of them and seriously question how we can deal with others, I fear that, in bestowing on animals this enviable promotion to *Zoo faber* in recognition of their genius, we might in fact end up neglecting the more discreet tools which take the form of social inventions and which are less likely to be perceived as inventions (especially because we relegate them to the distant realm of instinct or reduce them to often very simple functions). If I use the term 'technology' to describe these inventions, it is because Ursula Le Guin's wonderful idea of celebrating objects capable of containing things, of holding them together – a net, a basket, a knotted bundle – can also be applied to the notion of territories. Not only because, on an individual scale, they are 'homes' which bring together and shelter their occupants like the canvas of a tent but because, on a broader scale, each territory could represent a stitch in a net stretching across space and time.

But, in order to imagine this version of events, researchers first had to confront a considerable problem: that of the importance existing theories accorded to aggression.

5

Aggression

Early researchers, as I mentioned earlier, were powerfully struck by the vehemence of conflicts and by the pugnacity demonstrated by birds. However, even at an early stage, many of them questioned the true nature of such fights. They realized that what they were witnessing, and which had made such an impression on them, was in most cases simply threatening poses in the form of songs, displays, flapping of wings, puffed-out feathers, or mock attacks which, although sometimes extremely energetic, rarely resulted in dramatic consequences.

Howard was very clear on this subject. Too much importance, he wrote, had been attached to conflicts.[1] A bird can, for example, be peacefully feeding in a corner of its territory when an intruder arrives. Alerted to what is happening, he breaks off from his search for food and begins to walk or fly towards the intruder. At first, he moves slowly, but as he gets closer his pace gradually increases, and eventually he launches himself on the other bird, attacking him with his wings and beak and thus forcing him to recross the border. And at that point, Howard observes, the bird demonstrates a remarkable change of attitude and the attack ceases. He remains calmly on his side of the border, as though keeping guard, and shows no further interest in the bird which he had attacked so furiously just a few seconds earlier. Of all the fights observed, says Howard, it is clear that the end result is never to obtain the defeat of the intruder but, rather, to force it to retreat from a certain position. All fights begin with an infringement of borders and end when the intruder returns to his own side. Moreover, fights are much more frequent while territories are in the process of being established, a time when such encroachments are more likely to occur.

For Howard, the withdrawal of the intruder would be obtained as a result either of fear or of physical exhaustion, and consequently it would be wrong to attach too much significance to any injuries inflicted. These conflicts are, at most, he says, 'mere "bickerings" and lead to nothing'. In most cases these fights are largely 'formal': 'they are vestigial fragments of warfare that determined the survival of the species in bygone ages.' Moreover, fear and exhaustion are not the only factors which determine the nature and the intensity of the fighting: the most significant factor is position. The intensity and ferocity of the attack always depends on the position occupied by the bird while the fight is taking place. It is the respective position of each which therefore determines the propensity of the resident bird to fight. This is what led Howard to refer to the fighting 'as being controlled'.

It is remarkable that, in this extract, Howard identifies the two ways in which aggression would be understood by the majority of subsequent researchers. Firstly, these fights are more of a formality than anything else. And Howard develops the interesting hypothesis according to which the bird reconfigures inherited behaviours and rechannels these for the purpose of what is now this formalized warfare. Secondly, he observes that the attack is always initiated by the resident bird and that the intensity of the attack depends on the position occupied by the opponent. The majority of researchers ended up adopting one or other of these hypotheses, and in some cases both of them. The fact that the fight is a formalized activity was frequently observed. So, for example, in 1936, we read that, in territorial great-crested grebes, aggressive behaviour is demonstrated only by a few individuals, the majority tolerating conspecifics in the area around the nest. In 1939, in his observations of robins, David Lack noted that all encounters between rival males ended without a fight in the strict sense of the term, but with both birds singing instead. Such psychological and formalized fighting, said Lack, constitutes one of the most remarkable aspects of the behaviour of these birds – yet robins have long had a rather marked reputation for intransigence when it comes to territory. Nice herself emphasized, as we have seen, that in song sparrows the intensity of the posturing was inversely proportional to the seriousness of the encounter.

The other hypothesis, the one claiming that fighting is controlled and that it ceases once the intruder has retreated, not only received considerable empirical confirmation but would be further complicated by additional observations. Territorial conflicts, no matter how fierce they may seem, generally claim very few victims. But that is not all. Observations led to the conclusion that, paradoxically considering what is at stake, the outcome of such events is extremely predictable. The intruder is rarely victorious. In the majority of cases of territorial conflict, the power to win, as Thomas McCabe wrote in 1934, is always, or almost always, granted to the defender, in so far as he is in a position to defend his borders, whether by strength, by mimicking warlike gestures, or by the use of his voice. Nice comments on this theory by drawing a parallel with humans: the English proverb 'Possession is nine points of the law' suggests that ownership is easier to claim if the claimant possesses the object in question and more difficult if that is not the case. The claim made by whoever has possession would therefore have nine times more weight than one made by anyone else.[2]

Konrad Lorenz and Nikolaas Tinbergen confirmed this theory at the end of the 1930s, asserting that the defender of the territory will always fight much more vigorously than the intruder and is rarely defeated. This is what is referred to as the 'home-cage effect', where the 'owner' of a cage, when confronted with a new arrival, will always be victorious. Let us note in passing that the terminology provides the clue to its origin. In fact, a remarkable number of animals, from baboons to fish and including myriads of mice and birds, were subjected to the test of defending their 'territories', whether these were cages, confined spaces or aquariums. Researchers placed one of the creatures into the chosen space before introducing, some hours later, an unfortunate conspecific who, quite literally, did not know where to put himself. When the animal now designated as the intruder was introduced into the cage, the first occupant adopted all the behaviours researchers normally associated with dominance and the second displayed all the signs of submission. The outcome was so unmistakably linked to the order of occupation of the space that it was perfectly possible, only a short time later, to obtain a reversal of the situation with the same animals, simply by changing the order in which they were put in the cage. A considerable number of experiments with birds confirmed this result and demonstrated that the defensive vigour of the occupant is always stronger than the aggressivity of the intruder. In 1939, in a study of dominant behaviour in canaries, Hugh Shoemaker reported that a bird taking on a subordinate role in a neutral territory becomes dominant in its own territory. In 1940, Frederick Kirkman conducted experiments by moving the nests of black-headed gulls, normally 45 centimetres apart, closer together. He observed that aggressive behaviour switches sides depending on whether the same gull finds itself in the role of resident or intruder. Aggressive and self-confident when the nests are moved closer on its own domain, the gull becomes timid and hesitant when this takes place on the domain of another. In his book on aggression, Lorenz notes that there is a constant in territorial conflicts. The individual fights more vigorously if the combat takes place on his own territory. The increase in 'readiness to fight' is moreover not the same across the defended space but always increases, for the resident, as the middle and most familiar part of the territory is approached. And it diminishes in the same ratio in the intruder as it gets closer to that point. It is as though there is a gradient of forces emanating from the centre, and each of the protagonists involved is affected in relation to this.

This raises an obvious question, and it is one which I have been asking myself for some time. If the outcome is so predictable, why do animals still get involved in these conflicts?

Firstly, we need to remind ourselves that it is 'we' who know that the outcome is predictable. We know it because it has been noted by a great many observers who have gathered an extraordinary amount of evidence, based on the lives of thousands of birds, patiently obtained as a result of hundreds of thousands of hours of observation. There is therefore no reason why birds should make the same predictions as we do – at least initially. At the same time, it is also clear that they learn quite quickly from experience. In that case, the mystery remains unsolved. Of course, things are never completely set in stone, and we might suppose that the attempt is a kind of gamble (especially as there is not much to lose). Perhaps birds are open to the notion of unpredictability, to the idea that all situations are always, from the very outset, uncertain. Perhaps they are simply stubborn, like those tiresome people who will never believe in forecasts.

Yet this question, 'Why do they do it if the outcome is so predictable?', is perhaps not the right one to ask, given that it is based on a series of assumptions about competition, space and distribution within that space. I was often astonished, in the course of my reading, to see researchers subscribing to the idea that these conflicts are mere squabbles, that songs and mimicry are substitutes for fights, and that an intruder is only rarely victorious, and then, at the same time, finding these same researchers stubbornly engaged in trying to calculate the costs and benefits of these conflicts, defining benefits in terms of appropriation and costs in terms of injuries, risks, energy expended in clashes. There is clearly some contradiction here.

It should be pointed out that a great many economic models studying the distribution of animals in a particular space confined their theoretical horizons to the hypothesis of population control. But these theories, as Judy Stamps and Vish Krishnan point out, are based on a misconception, notably on the notion that the space involved in the acquisition of a territory is in some sense indivisible, and therefore cannot be shared.[3] According to Stamps and Krishnan, the fact that a considerable amount of research on territoriality (in particular on fish) takes place in the laboratory, in very confined spaces, is probably, and in all cases partially, responsible for this conception of space. Also, methods which consisted in removing residents in order to assess how quickly they would be replaced in a sense endorsed the underlying notion that each territory could be the subject of a victory, in the form of the radical dispossession of the resident. In reality, as we have seen, the results of the methods which corroborated this theory were based on the actively programmed disappearance of the resident. But even if a bird might succeed in gaining ground in the course of a conflict – an outcome which is always a possibility – this 'victory' does not involve the removal of the ejected rival. Yet this is exactly what such practices set out to do. In reality, conflicts between birds do not generally take the form of an all or nothing scenario. Given that the available space is a divisible resource, it is more often a matter of appropriating sections of territory. What happens on the borders, according to John Maynard Smith, the British evolutionary biologist and geneticist, should be regarded as bargaining and negotiation rather than as conflicts where the outcome amounts to a 'winner takes all' situation. In any event, even if this were the case – it is rare but can happen – and if the intruder were to end up discouraging the resident from remaining, the latter does not disappear for evermore. It is only when researchers get involved that the outcome is so grotesquely dramatic. And that changes everything.

Researchers, similarly intent on loading the dice in the territorial game, removed a resident. But, instead of killing it, they kept it in captivity, releasing it once a replacement had taken over its territory and observing what happened next. If we look only at the immediate result of what is supposed to represent the outcome of a conflict, it would seem that the original resident fails to retake control of his territory, and his attempts to do so throughout the day end in failure. But if we return to the situation in the course of the following weeks, as Beletsky and Orians did with red-winged blackbirds, it transpires that, two weeks later, 86 per cent of residents have reclaimed the whole of their territory, and 4 per cent have successfully retrieved some part of it. It would therefore seem – and this is the conclusion reached by Stamps and Krishnan with reference to this research – that being victorious in a fight does not constitute a crucial element of the process.

These observations, and others, seem therefore to point to another explanation of how to interpret the mystery of these conflicts with their predictable results. It might be assumed, and some observations point to this, that certain birds, with a great deal of determination, end up forcing a resident to concede part of the contested area, thereby gaining a section of territory on a space already occupied. It has indeed been observed that some birds, with remarkable obstinacy, provoke a resident, get chased away and keep trying. They are forced out on repeated occasions, but in the end the resident becomes disheartened and gives up. And all this without the need for any actual conflict, but simply with the aid of one of the oldest methods of warfare in the book – what we might call a 'war of attrition'.[4] It is therefore a matter not of forcing the resident out but of obliging him, by means of a subtle strategy of discouragement, to cede some space.[5]

Which means therefore that birds, or at least some of them, operate in a space which has little to do with theories of population control but, by negotiating how that space can be divided up, share it and tolerate further divisions. This was something Huxley sensed when he compared territories to elastic discs, capable of being compressed but only to the point where resistance to pressure occurs.

But does the solution proposed by Stamps and Krishnan to the question of why conflicts occur bring this question to a close? I think not. First of all, because it cannot take into account the existence of these conflicts in birds in situations where borders are very stable and attitudes to them somewhat rigid. For these birds, something else must be at stake. In addition, their response leads us to another question which has intrigued a number of researchers. Could claiming a section of territory in an area already divided up among a number of birds indicate that birds in fact want to be close to other birds? But why should they want this? Of course, many scientists have a ready-made answer: the most highly prized spots are the ones with most resources. It is not about being near other birds, but about being in the right location. But other ornithologists have demonstrated that this is not always the case, and that it is not quite such a simple matter. This is, we suspect, a much more interesting theory and one well worth returning to.

Yet another possibility might also be considered. In order to explore it, we need to turn our attention to other assumptions and return to the question of aggression. Territory, as we have pointed out, marks out distances. There are all sorts of reasons why an animal or bird might want, or need, to mark out distances, and the aggressive tendency is merely one among many others. But nevertheless, for a considerable number of researchers, this is the one that has captured their attention. And if aggression has continued to maintain its hold, and has excluded other possibilities so forcibly, it is largely because territory is always thought about in terms of competition. This is, for example, the very powerful theory advanced by Lorenz. Territory is determined by aggressivity, and this aggressivity 'causes' territorial behaviour. According to Lorenz, expressivity and mock attacks are, in a sense, ways of channelling and of ritualizing aggressive impulses, but they are nevertheless still part of these impulses and are always based on aggression. However, what appears to take the form of a conflict can be interpreted in a quite different way if we work on the assumption that aggressivity does not explain territory but, rather, presupposes it – or in other words that territory is the event through which the aggressive functions are reorganized into expressive functions.

Play provides a useful analogy. No one would suggest that, in animal play, aggressivity is present but reorientated. The fact that it can return when things get out of hand means not that it was already present in the form of an aggressive instinct, but simply that its deter-ritorialization failed at that moment – the situation shifted to being *something else*. Play borrows the *forms* of aggression, but aggression is clearly no longer the cause, nor is it even involved at all. What is happening in such moments is more a case of 'make believe', or 'let's pretend', forms of behaviour which exist in their own right and are what Souriau would call sublimation. This is an exaptation: behaviour which previously performed a function in the relationships between one creature and others is diverted and becomes a form of play instead. This is why play can be linked to play-acting and to the task of the actor playing his or her role. An animal can play his part well or badly, and there is an element of talent in these stories which is reflected in the use of the verb 'play' in relation to the role of an actor. From the moment we accept the fact that the territorial event has reorganized aggressive functions into expressive functions, Souriau's idea makes sense: the victor is not the best fighter but the best actor. The significance of what Nice shrewdly referred to when describing the different 'roles' assumed by her song sparrows also becomes clearer. These are roles which 'take over' actors, which take possession of them (something known to all good actors familiar with the risks of their profession), forces which can sometimes overwhelm them – and it is the same when animal play gets out of hand, when the animal is overtaken by his or her role, when aggressivity shifts from being formalized and resurfaces for real. And in territorial behaviours there is also perhaps an element of 'This thing is bigger than I am'. These extravagant and stereotyped poses, these endlessly repeated songs, these displays of colours are not only the expression of the forces at work – the magic of appearances, as I hear Moffat say, capable of operating at a distance in order to preserve a distance – but they also *activate* such forces. The philosopher Thibault De Meyer suggested that certain ornamental features could be compared to ritual masks in that they not only affect others, but they also affect those who wear them, they 'empower' them, he says. It is these, he adds, which trigger the release of power. He continues: 'Masks do not simply create powers *out of nothing*. They transform latent powers, bring them onto a larger stage, carry them into other territories.'[6]

Which leads him to suggest that art should be perceived as a game that seeks out and activates latent forces, previously existing only in an embryonic form. Diversion, activation, deterritorialization – in the service of what will become art, a domain indisputably linked to territorialization, as Souriau, Deleuze and Guattari, Adolf Portmann, Jean-Marie Schaeffer and many others have proposed.[7]

But the very fact of considering these expressive behaviours, these songs, poses, flamboyant choreographies, as forces and activators of force brings philosophers and ornithologists a step closer together. And, as a result, I find myself in a position to bring together the two questions still left open: firstly, why these conflicts, with their very predictable outcomes, occur and, secondly, why there is this apparent desire for proximity among birds.

The British ornithologist James Fisher observed that little attention had been paid to the deeply social dimension of territorial activities.[8] In effect, he says, biologists are more inclined to think of sociability and cooperation in what are called 'maintenance activities' such as feeding. But, according to Fisher, territory is a social activity which involves cooperation. Fisher's hypothesis goes against most of the theories of his time. It is based on a strong premise which, according to Fisher, is largely ignored in ornithology, notably the notion that birds are 'fundamentally social animals'. And it is that 'fundamentally' that is the crucial word here. Sociality is a rule, not an exception, and it permeates everywhere. And this completely changes the perspective. Territorial behaviour is not therefore simply aggressive behaviour kept in control as a result of social pressure but is itself fundamentally social, through and through. Thus, Fisher goes on, the idea, notably supported by Howard and Huxley, that displays are aggressive and that colouring serves to intimidate stimulated a considerable amount of research. But the resulting investigations neglected the social dimension of territorial behaviour and prevented people seeing them simply as a *marvellous exchange of genuine displays*. Fisher's thinking takes us back to the notion of territory as a space permeated with dramatic intentions, as drama, as the magic of appearances, magic in the sense of the effects of mock actions, but above all ways of appearing in a game which co-opts certain particular modes of attention. And this is indeed what we are seeing here. Fisher would pick up on an idea first proposed by the ornithologist Frank Fraser Darling. These so-called fights and these supposedly aggressive songs are 'social stimulations'. Basing his findings on his study of birds which live in colonies, and notably on herring gulls, Fraser Darling concludes that the co-presence of conspecifics stimulates these birds. Living together synchronizes reproduction cycles, making them more effective – here he takes up Allee's hypothesis according to which, below a certain population threshold, certain animals no longer reproduce. Fraser Darling goes further: such stimulation can be provoked simply by the presence of others but is *intensified* by the presence of a territory. Which leads Fraser Darling to the fascinating assertion that, for birds, one of the most important functions of territory 'is the provision of *periphery* – periphery being defined as that kind of edge where there is another bird of the same species occupying a territory.' Put another way, 'by pushing up against each other, rather than spreading themselves out, the birds are giving themselves peripheries.' He explains that, because it is 'a place with a focal point or two – the nest site and the singing post – and periphery',[9] territory enables two conflicting needs to be met at the same time, in that it offers security but also a border zone where things happen. And, according to Fraser Darling, this is what is happening here. The periphery is a central hub of life, or perhaps even of vitalization. It is the place where birds are most animated, both in the traditional sense of the term and also in the sense proposed by Thibault De Meyer. These are, to cite Thibault once more, 'devices to arouse enthusiasm'.[10] Referring to the observations of lapwings made by G. Rinkel in 1940, Fraser Darling explains that these birds, far from avoiding clashes, on the contrary seek them out: 'the males seemed to need them and the emotional stimulation they gave, and the birds sought opportunities for them.' Many other birds would also demonstrate similar tendencies, he suggests. A lot of activity goes on at the boundaries, and more often than not this animation is deliberate. And this is also what the territory and the extraordinary drama of all these games along its boundaries has to offer. As Fraser Darling concludes, an animal 'needs to go outside itself'. In animal life there seems to be 'a reciprocal responsiveness'.

It might therefore be assumed that these clashes which ostensibly amount to nothing are in fact akin to small dramas, endlessly replayed for their own sake, and provoking reactions. They stimulate both those acting them out and those to whom these performances are addressed. Because, in fact, territory exists only through territorialization and deterritorialization, since it is always in relation to entries or departures to and from the territory that it makes itself felt. Territories exist only through actions, which means that they are in fact performances, both in the theatrical sense and in the sense that their very existence depends on their being performed. It is these performances which 'affect' the territory and make it into an affected space, a space criss-crossed with affects. In a sense, the conflicts are put to the service of display, whether in the form of songs, dances, rituals, poses or colours. Such displays not only express emotions, affects, but also activate them. And this game, this performance which affects a particular place, which *constitutes* territory, cannot take place with fewer than two players – and, even then, two is scarcely enough.

Here too, territory is a *matter of expression* and a matter of social-ized expression. Or, more precisely, sociality is put to the service of territorialization, becoming part of its assemblage, repurposed for new usages. Territory is therefore, as Warder Clyde Allee sug-gested, a phenomenon which has more to do with ecology than with behaviour.

Counterpoint

If [scientists] tested the mental prowess of baboons with an array of social questions rather than with bits of plastic of different colour and shape . . . they might feel uncomfortably lacking in IQ.

George B. Schaller[1]

At the beginning of the 1970s, baboon primatology became an extremely controversial field, as researchers began to report observations from their field studies which contradicted previous thinking and accepted knowledge about baboons, and which consequently threatened to undermine the model faithfully illustrated by each baboon society. For there was indeed a 'model' of baboon society, with its relatively strict hierarchies of dominance, the clearly identified (and rather insignificant) role of females, open competition for resources, all the dimensions which somehow constituted what might be called species invariants. That model was beginning to come apart at the seams. The primatologist Thelma Rowell, for example, pointed out that the baboons she had been observing in Uganda since the beginning of the 1960s were not interested in competition, or in hierarchy, and that the influence exerted by females on any decisions was much more significant than had been thought. Her young colleague Shirley Strum reported that she was not seeing what she had been taught to see and described a society where dominance brought none of the advantages it was supposed to offer and where friendship with females represented a crucial asset for a male. How were such differences in social organization within one and the same species to be interpreted?

These perplexing variations initially gave rise to theories which questioned the validity of the scientists themselves, suggesting that, on the one hand, subjectivity and differences in method on the part of observers might be responsible for such discrepancies and, on the other, that research was still at too rudimentary a stage. Researchers themselves, however, relied on the idea that, with time, a more coherent approach would be reached. Some suggested that it was ecological conditions that were responsible for societies diverging from the norm in this way, a claim which did not, however, challenge the existence of such a norm.

The philosopher Bruno Latour came up with an alternative hypothesis. According to him, the sociological paradigm behind such research renders it incapable of taking into account the level of variation between baboon societies. For this paradigm is based on a definition of society as a mould into which the individual has to fit – this is what is called an ostensive definition of the social link. This mould would prove to be all the more rigid in that it was forged in the course of evolution. In an article written with Shirley Strum, Latour says that, if we want to understand the nature of a society, whether human or primate, instead of proposing a social matrix into which actors will need to fit or a social context which only sociologists are in a position to explain, we need to pay closer attention to the ongoing creation of associations, of links which *become* social. This sociology therefore adopts a 'performative' definition of the social link. Within this definition, actors continuously define what society is, both for themselves and for others. For society exists only in so far as it is constructed through the efforts of each of its members to define it. Rather than focusing on the social links established in the relationships between actors, we should explore how actors create these links and, in doing so, define what society should be – in other words, the social not as it *has become* but as it is *in the process of becoming*, as the philosopher William James might put it. What is interesting about this perspective is that it allows us to understand why Strum did not see what she had been taught to see and why her baboons stubbornly refused to illustrate the model to which they were supposed to conform. When Strum first arrived in the field, she set out to establish what kinds of questions the baboons might ask when embarking on a relationship with others. And it is these questions which subsequently guided her research. Consequently, from the very outset, Strum had adopted in her methodology a performative version of the social link. In subjecting the baboons to these questions, Strum learns that they are constantly negotiating, testing each other, guessing what the others' intentions might be or what they are going to do, creating alliances and endeavouring to find out who is allied with whom and, of course, trying to control or even manipulate the others. And these responses obtained from their observations of the baboons led Strum and Latour to conclude: 'And to the extent that baboons are constantly negotiating, the social link is transformed into a process of acquiring knowledge about "what the society is".' Put another way, 'baboons are not entering into a stable structure but rather negotiating what that structure will be.'[2]

As a result, the variety of ways in which the baboons organize their lives is not a simple product of external determinism, whether in the form of research conditions, ecological contexts or differences between one observer and another. Animals do not step into a society, any more than they step into an awaiting hierarchy or system of alliances, but instead explore, through experiment and investigation, in order to find out what their society might be. And, to do that, they must constantly test the availability and the solidity of alliances without ever having any guarantee as to which ones will hold firm and which will not work or will be broken off. This last observation leads Latour and Strum to suggest another contrast, this time between baboon societies and human societies. Where the former are complex societies, the latter appear rather to be complicated societies. The performative definition of the social link poses the question of how society can be achieved by focusing on 'what *practical* means actors have to enforce their version of the social bond'. What emerges when we try to answer these questions is one of the particularities of baboon society, notably that they have very few means of *simplification*. Where societies are *complicated*, such means exist. Human societies have access to symbols and material resources – such as contracts, guarantees, institutions, technologies, agendas, written undertakings . . . – which stabilize certain factors, keeping them constant and permitting actors to regard certain things, facts, elements, characteristics as *given*.

Baboons, for their part, must constantly relaunch their investigations and the negotiations which enable them to obtain their objectives. Indeed, if in the context of their social lives certain qualities of individuals are fixed, such as age, kinship or sex, the majority of the characteristics which allow them to predict or anticipate the behaviour of others must be continuously renegotiated in the context of relationships. As a result, baboons have complex sociality, which means that the solutions available to them to construct or repair their social order are never stable and must be constantly reactivated. In other words, in order to negotiate, they can rely only on their bodies, their social skills and the strategies they are able to invent.

In a text published some time ago, Gilles Deleuze suggested that instincts and institutions should be understood as serving the same purpose: they are, according to him, 'the two organized forms of a possible satisfaction'.[3] The institution, he adds, 'is always given as an organized system of means': sexuality finds satisfaction in marriage, just as 'marriage will spare you from searching out a partner, though it subjects you to other tasks.' This definition has the advantage of portraying society as 'inventive', in that it invents original means of satisfaction and institutions as positive: where law is a limitation of actions, the institution is a positive model for action. Society is all the more inventive, on the one hand, because the institution transforms the tendency simply by inventing the means to satisfy it and, on the other hand, because the institution cannot be explained by tendencies – 'the same sexual needs will never explain the multiple possible forms of marriage ... Brutality does not explain war in the least; and yet brutality discovers in war its best means.' It is worth noting that, in *A Thousand Plateaux*, Deleuze proposes a very similar idea, but this time in the context of territory. As we have seen, contrary to what Konrad Lorenz suggests, Deleuze and Guattari argue that aggression implies a territory but does not explain it.

I shall not discuss the contrast with instinct which Deleuze established in the text on institutions, since the latter would be of little help to us here. But, from the similarities between the analyses of the institution and of territory, I would like to retain two ideas. The notion of inventiveness first of all: the fact that, just as the institution cannot be explained by need alone, so territory cannot be explained simply by impulse. Territory is an invention which transforms needs and impulses into something else. More precisely in this context, and again returning to the intuition referred to by Fraser Darling, the territory is put to the service of certain possibilities of social action. Secondly, and this clarifies the first idea, the notion that the institution constitutes a model. Territory could play a similar role. The term 'model' is used here, not in the sense in which we have already encountered it – the *model* of baboon society which obliged baboons to conform to certain species invariants – but in the active, positive, performative sense, where the institution is, as Deleuze describes it, 'a social activity that is constitutive of models' capable of integrating 'circumstances into a system of anticipation',[4] and making it possible both to anticipate and to make plans.

Of course, territory is not strictly speaking an institution, but it could certainly fulfil a similar role to that of institutions in so far as it would be an invention which stabilizes certain dimensions, certain characteristics, which makes it possible to predict and anticipate. And to undertake certain projects successfully. Or, put another way, territory, in complex societies like that of birds, is an invention which allows complexity to be simplified, by ensuring the stability of some elements of social life and enabling its actors to predict, to a certain extent, how others will behave.

If this analogy is a relevant one, territory will therefore play a role similar to the one Shirley Strum ascribes to the hierarchy in place among female olive baboons. It would represent what she calls a 'structure'. In the everyday life of baboons, as we have seen, social transactions require constant work. Social grooming can, for example, partly fulfil the need for what might be called managing relationships and the creation of links of alliance or of friendship, but it is very much limited to a relatively small number of possible participants. The social cost and the stress involved in group life would be extremely high, Strum points out, if an animal did not understand, in advance, his or her relationships with others. Social life would be paralysed if the animals were forced to engage in constant negotiations whenever they needed to choose where to feed or to rest, where they should go, who they could approach and who they needed to keep away from. There would be no free time for basic needs and, undoubtedly, as Strum points out, no energy left to deal with any new challenges. 'Since complexity generates a variety of options', Strum observes, 'it is not surprising that individuals in a baboon troop disagree about what to do. These disagreements must be resolved because the group is constrained to move and act as a unit. Resolution requires negotiation. Therefore, managing the consequences of socioecological complexity is a serious daily challenge for baboons.'[5]

From this perspective, the female hierarchy is 'co-opted as primary structure'. It enables relationships to be stabilized and allows the animals to know what they can expect of others, how they are expected to behave, the potential alliances to be made and the reliability of these. The conservative nature of females, Strum adds, 'helps to keep this hierarchy relatively stable and predictable'.[6] Witness the fact that, if a male baboon loses in an encounter with another male, he might continue to contest the outcome throughout the day or even for a whole week. A female, in the same situation with another female, rarely challenges the results. The female hierarchy is not however totally rigid, since there are adjustments in rank between mothers and daughters, but these, according to Strum, do not generally affect the whole troop. By contrast, when changes occur in the female hierarchy as a whole, these can lead to outbreaks of aggression, sometimes of a highly violent nature, involving the entire troop. Group life can be put on hold for several days, and the continued instability may affect the group for weeks, and even months, afterwards. These periods of disruption are a powerful illustration of the need for a stable and predictable structure which enables the baboons to manage their daily life. The hierarchy is not therefore, as many scientists have claimed, a genetic characteristic but, rather, a transactional principle. 'The importance of structure is intuitively obvious when complexity and process are taken seriously. There are analogous arguments about structure from other fields. [In biological systems and for humans] a variety of theories argue for the benefit of structure to reduce uncertainty, minimize cognitive dissonance, build social relationships and facilitate social exchange.'[7]

It will, I think, be clear from the preceding pages that I am not keen on analogies, and I would certainly not want anyone to think that I was comparing baboons to birds. Birds are not baboons, particularly given the fact that it is difficult to make generalizations about baboons except for the fact that what we know about them is very much affected by the kind of questions we ask them. They do not constitute models – for themselves, for us or for birds – but they can create models in response to the challenges of life in a social context. What I hoped to gain by mentioning baboons here is in fact not so very far removed from what I am asking of birds: to open up our imaginations to other ways of thinking, to break away from certain routines, to highlight the effects of certain types of attention – what exactly is it that we decide to single out as remarkable in what we observe? And to make other stories possible. It is of course more difficult to open up these stories for birds than it is for baboons, given that the tendency to attribute so much to instinct, the ease with which organic changes can be referred to, their status as non-primates and, even worse, as non-mammals all serve to complicate matters somewhat. But we should bear in mind that, indeed, it was not particularly easy in the case of baboons either. What we know about them today should not make us forget the fact that, until the 1970s, they had, as Strum suggests, very limited options and that they were assumed to obey certain rigid determinisms which left them little room for manoeuvre. The fact that they can be regarded today as 'fur-clad sociologists'[8] is the result of hard work, of imagination and, more particularly, of other ways of paying attention.

But birds have benefited from certain advantages. Firstly, they have not been burdened with the onerous task of having to represent our origins and of providing a model for humanity.[9] In addition, as I have pointed out, ornithologists have from an early stage cultivated a comparative approach which has made them attentive to the many different ways in which birds organize their lives. Within the field, we see evidence of a constant tension between the desire to find a theory to unify the facts and the recognition that the sheer amount of variability means that no theory could ever hope to be anything but local. Finally, there is the extraordinary exuberance of birds themselves, their inventiveness, their remarkable capacity to convey the importance of territory and the beauty which is an intrinsic part of that importance. All of this must inevitably have favoured a certain attentiveness and a certain imagination. Those researchers who were susceptible to this therefore created space – sometimes no more than just a chink, but significant nevertheless – for stories which were less deterministic, stories which allow greater room for manoeuvre, both for birds and for those who observe them, stories which steer clear of any temptation to look for a model.

6

Polyphonic Scores

The architect Luca Merlini declared that architecture shapes human relationships.[1] We should, I think, strip this claim from its anthropocentrism. In their book *The Silent World*, Jacques-Yves Cousteau and Frédéric Dumas describe how, in the sea off the island of Porquerolles, they came upon an octopus village.[2] In it they saw what they took to be villas, one with a flat roof made of a broad slab of stone and held up by two stone and brick lintels and, in front of the entry, a rampart constructed of stones, fragments of bottles or pottery and crab and oyster shells. Since then, other villages have also been found. In 2009, in Jervis Bay, off the east coast of Australia, scientists discovered an octopus 'city' which they called Octopolis, and more recently, not far from it, another such city was identified and given the name Octlantis. Previously octopuses had a reputation for being solitary and generally unsociable. Such findings reveal that they are in fact capable of changing their habits or, more precisely, of accommodating, in a hitherto unknown manner, to an environment which has something to offer them. This is what Mike Hansell, a zoologist specializing in animal architecture, calls an 'ecological route', a term he uses to describe how the transformation of an environment carried out by living creatures can itself end up leading to modifications in terms of habits and behaviours, creating new ways of living and of organizing life.[3] What the octopuses did was to invent forms which in turn give shape to a society they were inventing in that same gesture.

Seen from this perspective, territories could be described as forms which create ways of being social and of organizing life.

We have seen that territories could be considered to play a role in the process through which couples are formed. Whether they stimulate the encounter, synchronize the birds' bodies, adjust psychological or physiological rhythms or forge relationships, territories are, as Souriau said when describing a tit's nest, 'mediatory works'. Referring to this nest, he writes, moreover, that it is not only a work of love but a 'creator of love', because it is in constructing the nest that the partners fall in love.[4] Territories therefore are forms which generate and shape affects, relationships and ways of organizing life within their confines. This might be deduced by observing certain birds which modify their matrimonial systems according to the territories in which they settle.

In dunnocks (other examples could be called on here, but I must confess to a particular personal interest in dunnocks),[5] matrimonial combinations vary considerably and include monogamy, polyandry, polygamy and polygyny. When a female chooses a large home range, defending it is a more challenging task. Often in such cases, the male will join other males and polyandry will prevail. If the range is more restricted in size, on the other hand, polygyny will tend to predominate. The home ranges of female birds are always exclusive, whereas the territories of male birds overlap when they live with the same female and they often cooperate in order to defend them. When a female establishes her home range, the male approaches and begins to fly around her, singing. According to observers, the male is engaged in exploring the female's range, but he is also setting up a *song territory* around her. If she agrees to establish herself within the sung territory of a single male, the couple will be monogamous. But she can equally decide to wander over two song territories, a choice which will lead to fights between the two males, who initially set about chasing each other, each one from the starting point of his own territory. After a while, the chases and song duels come to an end, with both males clearly accepting the intrusions of the other, an order of dominance is established and the territory becomes common to both birds. The two males appear to be on good terms and sing on the same perch. Conflicts will however flare up once more at the time when the female begins to lay, which, according to Davies and Lundberg, appears to reflect 'disagreements over how the copulations should be shared'.[6] In one of the cases observed, a young male, wandering around the territory of another bird, obstinately refused to give up. After being chased off on a number of occasions he ended up being accepted by the older male. The male of one of two neighbouring monogamous pairs was also observed venturing into the territory of the other couple and singing there, without meeting any serious resistance. After a few days, he became the alpha male over both territories, the other bird adopting the position of subordinate male. Dunnocks are relatively unusual in that the female establishes her home range first, choosing the location herself, a situation quite the opposite to what happens with robins, for example, where the female usually takes up residence in a territory already established by a male and, in the early days, follows him everywhere, probably in order to learn the limits of the territory. In dunnocks, the proportion of males to females is strongly affected by a high mortality among the latter. As a result, many males consequently find themselves condemned to celibacy. Dunnocks have, however, devised an extremely flexible organizational system which includes polyandric arrangements and allows a male bird to force himself onto an already established couple. The territory therefore shapes the way conjugality is organized – which does not mean it determines it but means, rather, that it provides a form on the basis of which birds can set about arranging their lives together. In other words, an invitation to explore formal possibilities.

But, more broadly, if we take into consideration the fact that the territory not only creates relationships within its own confines but also creates relationships with others, it is easy to see that, as the octopus cities might suggest, it could indeed have a 'founding' or 'instigating' function. From this perspective, territories would be forms which would generate social relationships, and even give shape to a society. Or, more precisely, they are forms which, in the majority of cases, renew the structure of society when this is confronted with new challenges, such as those associated with mating and reproduction. I would like to return once again to Fraser Darling's fascinating theory and in particular to a term he uses, and I quote him once again, in describing territory as 'a place with a focal point or two – the nest site and the singing post – and periphery'. The term 'periphery' draws attention to a highly significant aspect of territories which is that they are always *adjacent*. There is no such thing, or only in an exceptional case, as a territory 'in the middle of nowhere'. They always exist alongside other territories. They are always *neighbouring*.

At a very early stage in the history of research on territories, researchers, as we have already seen, came up with the hypothesis that birds might be mutually attracted to each other, something which would explain the phenomena Allee called 'contagious distributions'.[7] Yet, at the same time, this seemed paradoxical. Especially paradoxical, it should be pointed out, for those authors focusing on questions of competition and aggression, since these would justify the need for distance between conspecifics and aggression would ensure that this distance would be maintained. Proximity should therefore be seen *only* as an opportunistic decision to occupy the best sites, and would therefore result in these becoming saturated – a situation which would provide even further justification for competition. It is not impossible, moreover, to see how this impression of a saturated habitat might well have favoured the theory of population control.

For other researchers, however, provided it is accepted that aggression is intended to be largely spectacular and the fact that what is at stake is not, or at least not only, 'economic' – as Margaret Nice said with reference to her song sparrows – this proximity could have other motives. In 1937, Nice observed that the song sparrows tended to group their territories so that they formed a cluster – a collection of areas radiating out from a central point. Very early on, similar observations were emerging in Northern Europe. According to researchers observing these northern birds, conspecific attraction seemed to control the choice of territory. New arrivals were attracted by the songs of their fellow species and preferred to settle near birds who had already established their territory. Some researchers noted that new arrivals were sometimes happy with less than perfect territories provided these adjoined territories already occupied by conspecifics. It is of course difficult, as a human, to assess what constitutes a perfect territory. Experiments designed to look at this in a laboratory setting have succeeded in standardizing the conditions, but these are still not very reliable. On this subject, Allee noticed that a great many species which tend to aggregate in laboratory conditions do not do so in natural conditions and that, on the contrary, animals which seemed to want to aggregate when they are at liberty tend mutually to shun each other when in the restricted space of the laboratory.

Be that as it may, Judy Stamps points out that it is no coincidence that it was birds from northern latitudes which gave rise to this theory, since many of these are migratory and, as a result, annual fluctuations are very significant and variations in density much more marked than among resident species. This is because, on the one hand, when density is relatively low, as is the case at the time the first birds return from migration and when large areas are available, the effects of aggregation are much more noticeable. And, on the other, when a single population of birds experiences a brutal decline from one year to the next due to the vagaries of the migratory adventure, there is a surplus of available territories. Aggregation, in both these cases, is therefore not only more noticeable but can be interpreted as a choice, and not as the result of constraints arising from the pressure of a dense population.[8] Further supporting this theory, for certain species, is the fact that the order of appropriation varies from one year to the next. If it were simply a matter of food supplies, the first to arrive would choose the best territories, the next arrivals would opt for the next best quality, and so on, in a similar manner, year after year. However, it is clear that the formation of the cluster pattern reflects the location of birds already present when the next ones arrive, which varies from one year to the next.

While laboratory-based experiments prove not to be very reliable because of the effects of confinement, other experiments have been carried out in the field, in particular with a view to evaluating the attraction potentially exerted by the songs of already established birds on conspecifics in quest of a territory. When songs were played to pied flycatchers over loudspeakers, it appeared that the level of attraction increased in proportion to their intensity. Two other researchers, working on a number of red-winged blackbird colonies, investigated what is known as the 'Beau Geste' hypothesis, a strategy which refers to a tactic used by a unit of the French Foreign Legion which, by dint of making a lot of noise, succeeded in deluding the enemy as to its true numbers. In 1977, John Krebs proposed the theory that what seems to be the almost superfluous repetition of songs in territorial birds might serve to deceive new arrivals as to the true population density on the site, and therefore to discourage them from settling there. In the case of the red-winged blackbirds, however, it appears that the opposite effect is produced. The more singers there are, the more potential occupants turn up. But, for many species, it is clear that the potential to attract has its limits and that, above a certain threshold, a high density of population will produce the opposite effect. A deserted territory, in other words, is not attractive and nor is an overpopulated one. Other experiments would demonstrate that timing also has an influence. If songs are played once territories are well established, the tendency for other birds to try to settle there is reduced. When territories are in the process of being established the attraction remains strong. Borders are not mapped out in a landscape as yet undiscovered and undefended but are the result of social inter- actions involving individuals who will be living together on the same site. The birds do indeed choose a place, certainly, but what they also choose, and perhaps in certain cases what matters most of all, are their neighbours. Territory, as Fraser Darling believed, is therefore the creation of a neighbourhood.

Researchers have of course attempted to understand the reasons behind these choices in terms of practicality. It is not enough simply to claim, as Fisher did, that birds are *fundamentally sociable*, that soci- ality permeates all their behaviours. Selective pressure is driven by more concrete advantages. First of all, groups offer better protection against predators, particularly because of their ability to raise the alarm. Also, as mentioned earlier, the presence of a greater number of males is more likely to attract females. Another theory explaining why birds choose to settle near other members of their species con- cerns new arrivals, 'new' either because they come from somewhere else or because they are young birds just returned from migration. The latter do not have an intimate knowledge of the territory since they left it at an early stage in their development. These new arrivals make it their priority to seek out relevant information about the habitat. Nice had already explored this theory by observing that, when song sparrows born the previous year returned from migration, they established themselves near previously constituted groups, ignoring equally favourable and certainly less disputed habitats. Assessing food supplies and finding them takes time. It is all the more critical in the case of a first installation. Birds therefore have every interest in relying on those who already have that information and in settling as closely as possible to these. Animals living in close proximity can, deliberately or not, provide each other with a considerable amount of information. Moreover, birds have been observed to watch each other closely. Certain researchers have even advanced the theory that the promotional songs, display activities and rituals are reliable indicators of the state of health of a particular individual, and therefore of the quality of his territory.

Many observers have noted the curiosity shown by many birds towards each other. Researchers observing prairie warblers noted in 1978 that, out of 155 cases of intrusion, 122 were made with the sole purpose of watching the occupant eating, building the nest or feeding the fledglings, and noted that the visitor had clearly no intention of taking any food themselves during the course of the incursion. The presence of a neighbourhood seems therefore to offer a number of advantages. And, from this perspective, incursions would, at least for certain birds, be perpetrated less for aggressive purposes than from a desire to be informed.

It is, moreover, from the same viewpoint that Judy Stamps would suggest that conflicts on the borders are also deliberately provoked in order to obtain information. But, in this case, the information in question is not about the place and its resources but, rather, about the resident who is occupying it. When a new arrival envisages settling somewhere, he or she must interact with those who are already in residence in order to ascertain which territories have already been claimed. The simplest way of doing this is to approach the occupants and test their reactions. Any newcomer who plans to set up a territory will therefore be keen to provoke reactions, since this is the best way of learning what it is possible to do in the immediate vicinity and with whom. According to Stamps, intrusions at the borders are not therefore carried out with an intention to steal or in an attempt to appropriate space but are in a sense an investigation of the terrain and of the neighbourhood. The occupants are put to the test and this is a reliable way of getting to know them and an opportunity for the newcomer to introduce himself.

If territories are a way of establishing neighbourhoods, another hypothesis can also be envisaged. In the case of many birds, numerous observations have shown that gradually, as territories are established, as animals discover their limits and things settle down, conflicts begin to subside and relationships become more peaceable. In 1935, Frank Chapman observed golden-collared manakins on Barro Colorado Island, a man-made island in the Panama Canal. These birds clear an area of the forest floor to make 'courts', forming a cluster of sites which, because they are close together, are more readily visible to female birds. Referring to Chapman's work, Nice writes:

> The success of the *Manacus* system of courtship is based on a rigid obser-
> vance of territorial rights . . . This recognition of boundaries makes for
> law and order. No time or energy is lost in futile disputes or needless
> conflicts and the birds may devote themselves to winning the attention
> of the female, now the chief object of their lives . . . Under the normal
> conditions of courtship . . . the males are at peace with each other, not

because they are of a peaceful disposition and do not know how to fight, but because they are so well organized and observe the laws of court-life so rigidly that the occasion for conflict does not arise.[9]

At about the same time, the American ornithologist Alexander Skutch, describing the mild temperament of Central American birds, points out that, where birds have the whole year to adjust their territorial claims and settle their amorous disputes, they generally manage to negotiate these and reach an agreement without resort to violence.[10]

In certain species, it has been observed that conflicts with neighbours prove to be incompatible with courting rituals or with parental duties. Indeed, Judy Stamps advances the theory that the social style of a territorial grouping could influence the choice of females. Allee and his colleagues from the Chicago school had revealed that, in the case of sage grouse, whose territories are mating arenas (leks), the quality of relationships between males could have an impact on the preferences of female birds. A group of males was forced to move the site of its lek because of snow. This brought them into the vicinity of another group and, as a result, fighting continued during what would normally be the mating period. At dawn, the females arrived in large numbers. However, as the fighting was still going on, they withdrew to another location, which, according to the authors, corresponded to 'a mating place that was well organized and quiet'.[11] Moreover, among red-winged blackbirds, reproductive success was observed to be considerably better in groups where the male birds were familiar with one another, as opposed to groups made up of males who did not know one another. Stamps writes on this subject: 'From the female perspective, a group of males who had worked out mutually satisfactory social and stable relationships with one another might be preferable to an equivalent group of males who were still fighting with one another.'[12] If this theory is correct, she continues, 'then females should begin "male hunting" in territorial neighbourhoods in which the males indicate by their behaviour that they have already settled their disputes and are ready to devote themselves to courtship or the responsibilities of parenthood.'[13] As a result, females end up exerting pressure on the males to ensure they settle their conflicts as quickly as possible and coordinate their promotional behaviour. 'Cues that a neighbourhood is settled include coordinated countersinging among males or the absence of aggressive signals indicative of territorial contests.'

For living in a sung territory is also about accommodating to other birds, about being attuned to their songs. The composer and bio-acoustician Bernie Krause has been recording sonic soundscapes since the late 1960s. In most research carried out before then, he notes, researchers collected sounds in the way specimens were collected in museums, without taking account of the relationships that could exist between different species, or even different animal kingdoms. Krause himself, on the other hand, was looking for something else, and I would say that his perspective was very much in line with his role as musician and composer. He set out to understand how animals become attuned to each other and how they are attuned to their surroundings, to the wind and water, to other organisms, to the movements of vegetation. He wanted to find out how these animals create the silences which will contribute to the musical chord; how they share frequencies; how they attune to one another. 'First one bird, insect or frog might sing, then others when that one quits.'[14] What Bernie Krause refers to as 'collective vocal behaviour' is made particularly legible (for us) on the spectrograms in the form of an ensemble where it is possible to distinguish clearly the succession of channels: each participant – bird, frog, insect and mammal – forms their own temporal, frequency and spatial niches. And this creative arrangement tells a story.

> Where disparate groups of animals have evolved together over a long period, their voices tend to split into a series of unoccupied channels. So, each sonic frequency and temporal niche is acoustically defined by a type of vocal organism: insects tend to occupy very specific bands of the spectrum, while different birds, mammals, amphibians and reptiles occupy various other bands where there are fewer chances of frequency or temporal overlap and masking.[15]

All of which leads Bernie Krause to suggest neatly that the members of this 'acoustic collective . . . vocalize in distinctive kinship to one another.'[16] As a result of this segmentation into sonic niches, of these partitioned voices, through which conflicts linked to acoustic territories are settled, the birds' songs rarely overlap. Consequently, they become part of a new system, that of orchestration, not only in a strictly musical sense but also in the sense of a social musicality. Territories are orchestrations and melodic harmonies.

In the case of white-crowned sparrows in the San Francisco area, juvenile males establish their territory very early, well in advance of the reproductive season, and remain territorial throughout the year. Initially, these males have four different songs, but as time goes on they will favour just two of these, which are attuned to those of the neighbours with whom they interact. Observers have noted that their songs are modified as a result of contact with the descants of those neighbours.[17] This phenomenon of song matching is also observed in skylarks, and in this case the melodies become signatures indicating that the birds belong in the same place, the same neighbourhood, thereby enabling them to recognize one another. 'Singing like your neighbours' creates a community. Favouring a song similar to that of another bird within his own repertoire also fulfils a role which Michel Kreutzer calls 'addressing', enabling the singer to indicate to a neighbouring bird that this 'matched' song is indeed addressed to him.[18]

Over the course of our journey together, we have seen that thinking about territories also involves reactivating other meanings attached to words, expanding their semantic field, and deterritorializing them in order to reterritorialize them somewhere else: appropriation, possession, particularities, attunement, arrangements . . . All these terms now call for other modes of attention: they bring together other territories, intensify other dimensions, create new relationships, demand that other things be heard (silences and chords), other things be experienced (emotions, rhythms, forces, the flow of life and moments of calm), other things be savoured (things that are more intense, that carry most importance, the differences that matter). Those chords which denote good neighbourly relations between birds, which bear witness to a successful shared adventure, now invite me to introduce another term, also a musical one, which is that of the musical *score*. For territories are indeed musical scores. And, once again, the meaning expands to encompass two separate concepts, fortuitously expressed in French by the same word, *'partition'*: on the one hand, a musical score or composition made up of separate songs and, on the other, the process whereby a given space is divided into separate territories.[19] This double meaning suggests two different ways of inhabiting territory, a dual dimension which is both *expressive* and *geopolitical* at the same time. Territories map out networks of sound-based territorialities.

The idea that territories can be defined as what we might today call geopolitical forms of composition (bringing together) and of partition (dividing up) is not a new one and was first proposed by James Fisher. Many writers, including Nice and Lorenz, opted to describe territories as an expression of conventions – in other words, as forms which, when respected, exert a calming influence on collective social life and make it possible. Somewhat similarly, in his wonderful study of the figure of the diplomat, notably among wolves, Baptiste Morizot suggests that territories involve a system of placatory conventions, or, more precisely, that they are 'conventional devices for pacification'.[20] While it is true that there is evidence that, when birds defend a territory, they are not defending it against individuals from other species which do not have the same needs, it has been observed that, in many cases, intruders from the same species are tolerated as long as they are feeding but are driven away when they begin to perform displays or sing – as is the case, for example, with dunnocks. Territory codes everything. Baptiste Morizot observes that, when wolves cross a frontier, they stop their marking activities. Viewed in this light, territory becomes a place of good practices: from this point on, certain things are not done. It is no longer simply a matter of behaviour but, instead, an illustration of the most interesting aspect of the ecology of living communities, what Baptiste also calls *geopolitics*.

In the light of what we have seen so far, all of this makes sense for birds. As a system based on conventions, territory is the subject of experimentation by and about conventions: tentative attempts to establish where borders have been drawn, negotiations, provocations, challenges, a learning process, experimental forays, what is 'done' and what is 'not done'. The forms are respected. Like a series of tests in the process of creating the forms through which birds define what will from then on become their territorialized society, conventions are negotiated and then become established. And this theory is strengthened by the fact that very often, as we have seen, after a certain time things settle down and conflicts become less common. Birds can get on with other things. With the things that matter.

This is, moreover, what inspired Fisher's theory in 1954. He himself had noticed that songbirds often group together in establishing their territory and that the relationships between them and their neighbours are not greatly affected by competition.

> The effect of the holding of territory by common passerines is to create 'neighbourhoods' of individuals which are masters of their own definite and limited property, but which are bound firmly, and *socially*, to their next-door neighbours by what in human terms would be described as a dear enemy or rival friend situation, but which in bird terms should more safely be described as mutual stimulation.[21]

What Fisher calls the '*dear enemy effect*' will be the focus of a great many observations. And of a great many contradictions – not surprisingly given the inventiveness inspired by territory and by birds' penchant for indiscipline. It is indeed possible sometimes to observe what might be called the '*nasty neighbour effect*', which, in particularly competitive species, indicates that conflicts are far more marked with near neighbours, redefined as bad neighbours, than with strangers.

The 'dear enemy effect' can be seen when reactions in the event of an intrusion or the crossing of boundaries are notably less dramatic if the intruder is a close neighbour than if it is an animal from a more distant territory who is therefore unfamiliar. This effect is moreover often a dynamic one, since it generally establishes itself gradually (without being explicable simply as the result of habituation) and can change as circumstances are modified. This phenomenon has been particularly well studied in skylarks. According to ornithologists

observing these birds, the sense of familiarity generated by a neighbourhood allows them to avoid what the authors call 'role mistakes'.
Because they live together and have had experience of conflicts, and
of repeated conflicts, each of the partners in these neighbourhood
interactions gradually comes to establish relationships in which each
knows who the other is and what he might be seeking, the way he
behaves and what he owns – but should we still refer to 'conflicts',
or should we instead opt for a different term, such as 'a test based on
the sheer impressiveness of the spectacle'? Once these relationships
are established, birds are familiar with the roles each occupies and no
longer need to test each other in order to determine how they should
act and how others might behave.[22] Territory, therefore, might
indeed correspond to what Strum, referring to hierarchy, described as
a structure which allows interactions to be predicted. Moreover, the
'dear enemy effect' is established very rapidly at the beginning of the
season if birds were acquainted with each other during the previous
season, as is the case for the many birds returning to the same place
each year. The birds remember and, if there is disagreement on the
subject of a boundary, a short dispute will be enough to re-establish
it. Neighbours recognize each other: if a bird is played a recording of
a neighbour's song, he does not display much reaction. Unless, that is,
the recording is played from another location, for example from the
territory situated on the other side of the disputed border. In that case,
the bird treats his neighbour as a stranger. One of the most plausible
hypotheses, according to ornithologists, is that the bird did indeed
recognize the song and successfully identified the bird in question.
But the latter has changed territory and therefore his motives are
different, and roles and relationships are no longer the same.

Another, very similar, hypothesis can however be envisaged to
explain the 'dear enemy effect'. If the neighbouring bird crosses the

borders, the resident bird may assume that there is some kind of dispute and, since the neighbour already possesses a territory and therefore does not need to claim another one, that either the female bird or the food source is targeted. There is therefore less at stake. But this 'dear enemy effect' is not a rigid one. First, it requires a certain amount of time to become established. Male skylarks return to the same place each year, but the effect of familiarity is undoubtedly wiped out during the non-territorial period and the birds have to renew their acquaintances with their neighbours from the previous year. The effect can also disappear at certain times and in particular at the end of the first period of reproduction. At this time, females are again sexually receptive and ready to engage in extramarital relationships. In such cases, the 'dear enemies' become 'non-trustable familiars'.[23] In addition, the fledglings of the first clutch are busy making their first attempts at flying and borders are repeatedly crossed, resulting in a certain amount of disruption and of agitation – or in opportunities to reactivate territorialization. In the end, there is nothing quite as turbulent as a territory.

Up until now I have made very little reference to relationships between different species. It is true that territorial behaviour can sometimes be directed to other close species, although territories more often overlap as though they were different territorial spheres. But there are sometimes exchanges, 'captures', entanglements that are far more complex than a simple and ostensibly relatively indifferent juxtaposition.

Although territorial behaviour within multi-species groups has been recognized for some time, it seemed to be limited largely to species living in very specific ecological conditions and notably those found within the forests of South America.[24] So, for example, in the Amazon basin forests of south-eastern Peru, there are colonies of insectivorous birds often including a dozen different species, each represented by one family. The territory is shared and defended collectively against neighbouring colonies, although in a relatively unaggressive manner, with the majority of interactions conducted through songs. Evidence shows that the groups are stable and that certain species, notably certain species of batara, form the core. The bluish-slate antshrikes give the rallying cry for the morning gathering – the birds sleep in separate areas within the territory – and direct the group's movements, and the dusty-throated antshrike takes over in the absence of the former. In the rare instances of conflict with another colony at the borders, it has been observed that each member of the group communicates only with conspecifics within the other group – and where these are not present shows no further interest in the conflict. The astonishing organization of these multi-species colonies suggests that these are the product of a long history of co-evolution. Not all species join groups, and a group can only function where the techniques employed to obtain food supplies are similar, given that the group imposes a certain way of foraging and each individual must be able to move in a way which is compatible with the rhythms and movements of the others. This suggests that the colonies are selectively made up of ecological rivals sharing the same way of life, the same resources and the same habitats. In theory, competition should be intense. This is not, however, the case. Researchers have noted the existence of measures in place to reduce multi-species competition, with each species adopting different ways of feeding on insects: the sizes of their prey differ, as do the techniques used to track them down and the height at which the insects are hunted, ranging from close to the ground for some species to higher up, under leaves or below branches for others. Similar observations have been reported in many tropical forests with different species – mainly bataras – taking on the crucial role of guides in charge of the morning gathering, making contact calls, raising the alarm, sometimes even sending out false alarm calls when kleptoparasite birds attempt to intervene and to steal food by taking advantage of their strength. Vigilance with regard to predators in areas where birds are relatively visible, where there are few hiding places and where feeding methods leave birds with little time to detect danger seems to be a crucial aspect of these skilfully organized cohabitations. This theory leads me to think that these birds have collectively invented particular modes of attention: they have learned to pay attention to those who are most skilled at being attentive.

It has long been thought that the rarity of these ecological circumstances might explain the fact that this phenomenon is rarely found elsewhere. Of course, birds of different species can indeed 'do things' together, but this has nothing to do with territories. Finn's weavers, for example, nest collectively in trees also inhabited by other birds, notably drongos. The drongos' role is clearly a protective one and the weavers have been observed to adopt the same behaviour as the drongos towards predators.[25] The American ornithologist Bernd Heinrich noted that a great many species of birds join the winter flights of tits. These include golden-crowned kinglets, red-breasted nuthatches and downy woodpeckers. He also observed that the latter species do not normally gather together except in the presence of tits. The tits are often numerous and noisy and are also the most conspicuous among passerines. This makes them the most visible target. Heinrich describes how he has difficulty finding golden-crowned kinglets when he wants to observe them: they are rare, very discreet and often invisible in forests. Instead, the researcher relies on tits and on their talents for companionship and seeks them out in order to find his kinglets. By so doing he is expanding the multi-species network represented by the tits, now co-opting a human scientist. Which leads the scientist in question to formulate the theory that the golden-crowned kinglets use the same strategy of hybrid association, locating each other by joining the tits. During particularly cold winters in the forests of Maine, it is essential for the kinglets to be able to stay close together, if only in order to spend the night together.[26] 'The availability of body warmers at dusk cannot be left to chance; losing only one or more members per troop might doom the rest to freezing to death on some cold nights, especially after a day of poor foraging.' This idea of birds sheltering within a territory sung by others in order to ensure that, at some point or other, they can be tracked down by other birds of their own species is certainly an appealing one. And it gives another meaning to the notion of public transport.[27]

But a sung territory which welcomes other species does not quite amount to a collective territory. In reference to the recordings made by Bernie Krause showing the interest apparently displayed by a wide range of different animals in the 'partitioning' of sound fields, we have already pointed out that research on what I would call expressive cosmopolitics has been more infrequently carried out, with researchers instead focusing more on relationships within the same species. This choice is undoubtedly linked to the fact that the study of relationships between different species has tended to confine itself within the sphere of an ecology which has focused, in terms of interdependency, largely on what Fisher refers to as 'maintenance activities', such as feeding and seeking protection from predators. Collective displays of animals from different species, in the context of territories, tended moreover to support the idea that competition would predominate, even more than in conspecific relationships. From this point of view, if different species of territorial birds sing in the same place and are in competition with each other, it might be expected that each would try their best to fill the available sound space, even to the extent of scrambling or rendering inaudible the song of other birds – a process referred to as 'signal jamming' or 'signal masking'. This is indeed often the case. And when one bird begins to sing before another bird has finished singing, this is generally interpreted by the birds themselves as a display of hostility and usually provokes confrontational interactions. Musical cooperation would therefore be reserved rather for pairs of territorial birds, when the members of a couple join forces, and I am again referring here to the theory advanced by researchers, to defend a food supply, advertise the qualities of a particular individual and maintain the link between mates. We know moreover that musical cooperation requires practice, and scientists have put forward the theory that the quality of the performance reflects at the same time the fitness of the two partners, the quality of their commitment as a couple and the time they have spent together. In recent years, however, it has been possible to record and analyse the choral songs not just of couples but of tropical territorial groups of birds made up of a few individuals, always of the same species. According to observers, such choruses contribute to the cohesion of the group and to the defence of the territory and may also provide an indication of the quality of commitment of those involved. Collective territorial choruses might indeed exist, but this phenomenon was thought to be limited to groups of birds of the same species. Except that this turned out not to be the case.

An Italian bio-acoustician, Rachele Malavasi, and a specialist in sound ecology, Almo Farina, returned from the forests of the Latium region of Central Italy with the joyful news, for anyone interested in expressive cosmopolitics, that interspecific choruses do indeed exist. These researchers based their work on two hypotheses.[28] The first of these examined whether the 'dear enemy effect' might also be present in interspecific communities of territorial neighbours. If this theory is correct, it would underpin the second, relatively recent theory, which suggests that seasonal interspecific communities of European birds are not, as has long been believed, made up of anonymous individuals. According to this long-held perception, the fact that these groups were composed of 'anonymous individuals' rendered any form of cooperation virtually impossible. The two researchers therefore chose to carry out their study on a site in the woodlands of the Latium region where they expected to hear choruses of birds of different species at specific times of the day. A dozen species were identified – robins, chaffinches, firecrests, short-toed treecreepers, winter wrens, great tits, woodpeckers and other passerines, seven of which featured in all the recordings. Do these constitute choruses? If so, it should be possible, notably by analysing sonograms, to identify a particular feature of coordinated choruses: birds avoid signal jamming while at the same time allow themselves to deliberately overlap each other's songs. These choruses, if they do indeed prove to be so, would represent the expression of neighbourly relationships between different species and would have evolved in a similar manner, or in response to functions similar to those of coordinated duets between pairs of birds.

The researchers chose to obtain their recordings at a time when territories had already been established, where any effects of the 'dear enemy' approach would be already firmly in place. Bird songs are at their most intense at dawn and at dusk. They chose the latter period, because it seemed likely to provide the most favourable conditions. Indeed, according to the literature, there is a risk that dawn may well be the moment when birds tend to have more individual reasons to sing and when songs are motivated more by competition. For each recording, the two scientists chose to analyse the richest eight consecutive minutes from each sample, largely because these were likely to correspond to periods when most of the species would be participating in the chorus. They discovered that birds do not avoid overlapping – although they could have chosen to do so – and could sing during the period when other birds were singing. Yet these overlaps were deliberately designed to overlap as little as possible with the spectral structure used by the other birds. And when the overlapping songs occupy the same frequency range, the singers were observed to adjust vocal production on a very short temporal scale. There is therefore neither cacophony nor intervals of silence but, instead, a score made up of different parts and reprises. These choruses are therefore evidence of genuine coordination between the birds and demonstrate the existence of a strong association between them. The fact that they succeed in attuning their overlaps without causing signal jamming is because each has experienced the songs of the other species in the group and has learned their spectral structure.

Inspired by the honest signals theory, the authors suggest that these choral performances should be considered as an active demonstration of the qualities of the chorus members, qualities which they express as though for the attention of 'eavesdroppers', whether in the form of a possible rival or a potential mate: not only are they in good physical condition but their talent implies that they have available time and energy to learn and have been able to practise together. The fact that birds do not avoid overlapping, which would be possible by singing only during the so-called refractory periods when other birds are silent – 'It's my turn now' – shows that this is an actively organized coordination. With just one exception: the European robin adopts the rule of a 'segregated acoustic pattern', waiting until other birds have finished singing before beginning to sing himself. But, according to the two researchers, this was predictable given that the robin is a solitary species with very marked territorial behaviour. I have already hinted that the theory about the robin's penchant for solitude would eventually resurface after a long period of dormancy, and I think we can see evidence of this happening here. But, at the same time, the robin's attitude makes it all the more convincing that birds could just as easily have chosen to use the intervals of silence following other birds' songs to sing themselves, given this was clearly a possible option. Controlled temporal overlap is therefore not the result of a lack of silence but, rather, evidence of a genuine *musical score* along the lines of a polyphonic composition.

These coordinated songs will find themselves assigned functions which have already been referred to in other contexts. Their role could be, for example, to suggest the stability of the group to potential intruders. For females, they indicate that male birds are capable of establishing cooperative relationships and of holding on to the territory in the long term. They may also perhaps play a role in social interaction and favour the establishment of social networks. These theories, the researchers insist, are not mutually exclusive. In the context of expressive cosmopolitics, it is inevitable that many assemblages must have been undone and reassembled, that many other deterritorializations and reterritorializations will have taken place, other scores been played, other arrangements envisaged. The birds of each of the species involved clearly have their reasons for singing and for doing so with others, and these are also undoubtedly not necessarily the same in each case. And there are unquestionably other elements at play here: elements of taste, of beauty, of rapture, of exaltation and of newly unleashed powers, of courage, of importance and of enthusiasm, of respect for forms, of magical harmonies, or of celebrations at the close of day – we are alive! As my friend Marcos reminded me, has it not after all been said that birds elevate the created world into a state of praise? Or, perhaps we should add, that they transform creation into a state of grace.

This research from the Italian forests moves me precisely because it allows this grace to be felt. Because the two researchers felt, and make others feel, that these songs should be praised. It moves me because it succeeds in focusing awareness on modes of attention, in learning how to be in tune with these and to attune them to each other. Attention not only to the songs and to the magic which guides and accompanies them, but also to the scientific conditions which allow this magic to be perceived – choosing the right moment, the right time of day, the relevant intervals that allow overlaps to be understood. It is about finding the theories which are more in tune and better in tune, both in the sense of being attuned to a richer and more diverse reality and in being more closely attuned to birds and to their performances than was the case with previous theories. It is the realization that a territory is an ensemble made up of many different powers. And knowing how to respect these. Creating a territory means creating modes of attention, or, more precisely, it involves putting in place new regimes of attention. These two scientists succeeded in learning how to pay attention in the way birds pay attention to each other. By stopping, listening, and listening again. Here, now, something important is happening, something significant is being created.

And this is no doubt one of the reasons why our era might be placed, as Donna Haraway proposes, under the sign of 'Phonocene'. It means not forgetting that, if the earth groans and creaks, it also sings. It means not forgetting too that these songs are in the process of disappearing, but that they will disappear all the more rapidly if we do not pay attention to them. And with them will also disappear a multiplicity of different ways of inhabiting the earth, of the inventiveness of life, of arrangements, melodic scores, fragile appropriations, ways of being, things that matter. Everything that goes into the making of territories and everything created by territories which are dynamic, rhythmic, lived and loved. And inhabited. Living our era by calling it 'Phonocene' means learning to pay attention to the silence that a blackbird's song can bring into existence; it means living in sung territories but also acknowledging the importance of silence. And acknowledging, too, that what we risk losing, because of our failure to pay attention, will be the courageous singing of birds.[29]

Counterpoint

> Outside a song is taking shape. A few trills at first and
> then a pure, virtuoso aria which drives darkness away.
>
> Caroline Lamarche[1]

It is early February. For several days a blackbird has been coming into the courtyard in front of my house. He pecks at the few remaining seeds that the winter has left on the vine growing over the façade, but I get the impression this is merely a pretext. Or at least an opportunity. The bird is already caught up in something else. He has chosen a tree a little further down the lane, and he keeps watch there for long periods, perfectly still. I can see him from the window of my study. He watches, sometimes raising his small head up towards the sky. He does not distract me. On the contrary, he focuses my attention on what I am doing – on my writing. I am writing in his company. In the evening, when I go out with Alba, my dog, for a final walk, I can hear him practising his song, still quite discreetly. I cannot see him, but I know he must be on a roof, somewhere close by. He sings calmly, almost mechanically, like someone practising scales. In the silence the song is like a small light glimmering in the darkness. The winter is not yet over and there is snow forecast for tomorrow. But I know that, soon, the sun will rise with this blackbird and that each morning I will wake up to find myself living in a sung territory. I can already sense that a new story is beginning to take shape. The blackbird is here. And I am glad that it is through the grace of his presence, and in his presence, that the last lines of this story are being written and that another one is beginning. May he be thanked for it.

POSTSCRIPTS

A Poetic of Attention

'Slow down: work in progress'

Vinciane Despret listens to the blackbird singing and to ornithologists thinking.

Countering the trend of a science in a hurry to promulgate great universal laws, as in physics or chemistry, and to jump, far too quickly, to the conclusion that nature is simply a jungle where the notion of the survival of the fittest holds sway, Vinciane advances tentatively, one step at a time. She observes the ideas of ornithologists in the same way that these observe birds. She calls for researchers who are ready to observe tirelessly, who are not afraid to hesitate or to suspend judgement, and who take the time to allow the smallest differences to emerge, the most modest particularities to become apparent. Taking infinite care, Vinciane explores the labyrinth of their theories. She is on the lookout for ideas, hunting them down, and, as she writes, we see them appear, evolve, disappear, and sometimes reappear once again. There is a kind of ecology of ideas at work here. Vinciane pays attention to whatever attracts the attention of these scientists: a supercharged attention which enables the subtle diversity of things, of beings and of ideas to express itself.

The most interesting biology of our time is one which politely focuses on the smallest details, the most minuscule particularities. Differences are no longer wiped out by statistics but, on the contrary, are invited to speak for themselves. The living world is full of exceptions to the rule; life evolves only by diverging from a central equilibrium. Sensors with previously unknown levels of precision, new techniques of identification and long-distance tracking allow us to analyse statistically an extraordinary body of observations previously relegated to the ranks of mere anecdote. Today biology is capable of revealing individuals and, even better, personalities, life histories, genealogies, complex social relationships, learning processes and the transmission of experience and of cultures.

Biologists are turning into biographers and biology is becoming a literary undertaking.

In praise of slowing down

By teaching us patiently to observe all the living creatures around us, those naturalists summoned by Vinciane open doors for us, expanding our imaginations, multiplying perspectives and the opportunities to enrich the world. Biology is a slow science. There is a genuine grace in advancing slowly in this way, on tiptoe, taking small steps to avoid trampling on things and on creatures. It is a science focused on individual variations which enchants the world by delicately and elegantly unfolding for us other ways of living and new ways of thinking. And, as a result, the world becomes more complex, more difficult to grasp, certainly, but infinitely richer and more fascinating . . .

But this poetic of attention is also a matter of politics, for if this biology is indeed a science of wonder, it is also a lesson in how to live. Through it we can glimpse hitherto unimagined ways of living together, of cohabiting, of spending time with each other and of sharing spaces and stories with neither exclusion nor conflict. In short, it invites us to imagine new perspectives which will enable us to envisage a new form of alliance with the natural world.

And the starting point for all of that might mean agreeing to be awoken at dawn by a blackbird's song ... perhaps even looking forward to it, hoping to hear it and being grateful for it ...

Stéphane Durand

Gathering up the Knowledge which has Fallen from the Nest

'A book about birds! That will be bucolic, uplifting, delicate, as cosy as a nest.' But, no, there is not the slightest hint of sentimentality here: Vinciane Despret's book is full of differences of opinion, disagreements, ongoing debates. 'So, we might say, we were well and truly taken for a ride. It wasn't a book about birds, but about the scientists who talk about them, about scientific controversies.' But, no, there is no denying it, this is indeed a book about birds, first of all because it is a book *for* birds. Not in a militant sense ('Stand up for birds!' – Yes, indeed, but who would disagree?). More in the way we might say 'It's for you' when we give someone a present. And, yet, birds cannot even read.

The sense that this was indeed a gift intended for birds themselves struck me a few days after I had read the manuscript. I was reading a novel in the sun. I heard a bird singing. I felt pleased with myself because I was able to identify the song as that of the chiffchaff. Yet something was troubling me, and it was the realization that an ability to name the species was in fact more or less the extent of my knowledge. It seemed pathetic, insulting even.

Yet at the same time I became aware of a new sensation with the realization that this song was humming with a thousand meanings, redolent with references to functions which I could not even begin to understand, like hieroglyphics on a palimpsest scratched out and rewritten many times. And it was reading *Living as a Bird* that gave me that clear sense of the existence of multiple non-hierarchized meanings: what I had heard was simply a bird's song, and yet human minds have used their finest resources of intelligence in order to capture its meaning, unveiling theory after theory, arguing and debating, without being able to reach any agreement. The three notes of the chiffchaff's song are literally overflowing with hundreds of pages of ornithological arguments, of disagreements, of daring theories. Just three little notes and yet the collective intellectual prodigies of the world are still engrossed in exploring them and have yet to have their final say.

In my philosophical studies and in my writing, I often try to redescribe the living by drawing attention to their rich heritage, through the density of their evolutionary history, the significant aspects of their lives, their interwoven stories, their combinatorial freedoms. It is a matter of enriching the living with the murmur of their ongoing evolution which embeds within them the strata of an infinite, multi-faceted historicity, capable of responding to the present in order to reinvent life. This is my way of trying to give back to the living their ontological dignity, the irreducible grandeur that I sense without fully understanding. In this book, Vinciane Despret maps out a different trajectory, one more clearly understood through contrast and which ascends to the same summit, but via a different route. For she has crammed into every aspect of living behaviour another version of the infinite, one that corresponds to the ongoing human debate, to the endless hermeneutics, to the dissension between great minds; and in so doing she has succeeded in enriching her subject in a way that modifies it more powerfully than any traditional ecological or evolutionary arguments.

In order to do this, Vinciane Despret has discreetly brought about a change in the way science examines opposing ideas. In fact, not all theories have the same status in the history of science. Explanations, in the way these are understood in the traditional natural sciences, are expected to take a particular course, with each new theory over-shadowing the preceding ones. This happens schematically, so that on each occasion the most recent cancels out any predecessors. For example, when Darwin's theory of evolution appeared on the scene it cancelled out all the other theories from the likes of Lamarck, Buffon and Linnaeus. Yet, on the other hand, we know that, when we analyse a work of art or a novel, interpretations are very different indeed, combining, reticulating, mutually enriching each other. The latest one recomposes, relativizes and reconfigures the preceding interpretations but is part of the same fabric. In some respects, an intermediary process is taking place in the social sciences: when a new idea emerges on the origins of the French Revolution or the end of the Spanish Golden Age, certain arguments are dismissed, but in most cases the new proposal ends up becoming part of the edifice which brings them all together, altering it in the process. It is in this middle ground, the non-Popperian one of historical sciences,[1] that Vinciane Despret's work quietly and without fanfare establishes a new home for the science of animal behaviour. We continue to evaluate theories and ideas, eliminating the least credible and the least interesting, but allowing the others to interlink, sometimes forming a hierarchy but without the most recent arrival cancelling those already in place.

In so doing, Vinciane Despret sets out not to create new knowledge about birds but instead to transform the hitherto epistemological status of that knowledge. Previously firmly lodged in the uncom-promising grip of explanations, governed by the competitive and subtractive logic typical of mainstream natural sciences, she has relocated it and incorporated it into the multicoloured and cosmopolitan marketplace of interpretation, one characterized by cooperation and integration.

She has substituted an approach based on explanations for a hermeneutic one. This is one of the unusual aspects of this little book which sets out to clarify without seeking to explain, which draws on the various ornithological attempts at explanation in order to defuse them as 'scientific explanations' – that is to say, definitive and exclusive ones – and to hijack them, in the way a plane might be hijacked, transforming them instead into *interpretations* which accumulate and adjust to each other instead of cancelling each other out. Explanations stifle each other by competitive exclusion, whereas interpretations interlink, play with each other (like wolf cubs play together). Here, explaining an aspect of animal behaviour is not about finding the true law of nature, the primary cause, the ultimate equation, but instead about setting the scene for an ongoing debate on all possible meanings. Traditional history of science is often a graveyard for dead ideas. In this book, it is a flourishing domain.

By following this route, it is through the ongoing human debate on the meaning of their behaviours that the living demonstrate that they are not composed of stupid and ignorant matter but that they are in fact much more than that, a *supermatter* with powers that are beyond our understanding, yet without being supernatural.

The book is not therefore aimed at us. It does not conclude with lessons on humans drawn from observations of scientific controversies. Birds are not held up as a mirror for humans; the subject is not pinned on to planet '*Homo*' by the gravitational force of anthroponarcissism (like each time humans talk about animals only to end up talking about themselves). On the contrary, here birds are enriched with all the resources of human discussion: the relationship of means to ends is reversed. It is no longer a matter of salvaging the delicacy of the nightingale or the cunning of the crow as heraldic devices to enrich human symbolism, but one of kidnapping the investigation, science, human thinking, in order to enrich non-human life.

This gives deeper dimensions to the experience of a bird's song, to the three notes of the chiffchaff. Animals no longer need to be capable of handling tools, of counting, of being 'more intelligent than was thought' (the classic strategy of attempts to re-evaluate them) in order to have inexhaustible depths. The most stereotyped behaviour, the most unsophisticated song, is already more complicated to interpret than our capabilities permit. It has the infinite depths of Talmudic debate. Living creatures are overflowing with acephalous intelligence.

What a magnificent magic trick! If humans exhaust their intelligence trying to understand the three notes of the chiffchaff's song, it is because those three notes, by an absurd syllogism, are more intelligent than they are (in a *different* meaning of intelligence – that of simple and unfathomable primitive mysteries).

Baptiste Morizot

Notes

Counterpoint

1 E. Souriau, *Le Sens artistique des animaux*. Paris: Hachette, 1965, p. 92.
2 Ibid., p. 34.
3 Bernard Fort would moreover give the title 'Exaltation' to one of his electroacoustic compositions based on the songs of skylarks: *Le Miroir des oiseaux* (Groupe de Musiques vivantes de Lyon, produced by Chiff-Chaff records).
4 D. Haraway, *The Companion Species Manifesto: Dogs, People and Significant Otherness*. Chicago: Prickly Paradigm Press, 2003.
5 Baptiste Morizot invites us to take a similar direction with his conception of tracking as an art and a culture of attentiveness which encourages us to re-examine the ways in which we cohabit with other species as well as with humans.
6 E. Viveiros de Castro, *Cannibal Metaphysics*. Minneapolis: Univocal, 2014, p. 196.
7 D. Debaise, *Nature as Event: The Lure of the Possible*. Durham, NC: Duke University Press, 2017, p. 2. The speculative question which runs through his work, 'how to grant due importance to the multiplicity of ways of being within nature', is based on the acknowledgement of the ever-present influence of what Whitehead called the 'bifurcation of nature', the effects of which are still being felt, notably in the denial of plural forms of existence within nature. The 'bifurcation of nature',

which determines our modern experience of the world, refers to a way of understanding for which our experience reveals only what is apparent, whereas the elements necessary for the process of discovery and understanding are always hidden and must be found elsewhere. As a result, nature ends up divided into two distinct systems.

8   In the work of Louis Bounoure the expression 'cosmic factors' recurs repeatedly to indicate, in particular, the lengthening of daylight and the modification in temperatures. L. Bounoure, *L'Instinct sexuel: étude de psychologie animale*. Paris: PUF, 1956.

Chapter 1   Territories

1   This is, for example, the hypothesis developed by Ernst Mayr, 'Bernard Altum and the territory theory', *Proceedings of the Linnaean Society*, 45–6 (1935): 24–30.

2   I am referring here to Margaret Morse Nice, 'The role of territory in bird life', *American Midland Naturalist*, 26/3 (1941): 441–87, and to David Lack, 'Early reference to territory in bird life', *Condor*, 46 (1944): 108–11.

3   T. Birkhead and S. Van Balen, 'Bird-keeping and the developments of ornithological science', *Archives of Natural History*, 35/2 (2008): 281–305, at p. 286. I would add, since we are on the subject of appropriation, that the work of these two writers involves highlighting this form of amnesia, very prevalent among scientific ornithologists when it comes to the knowledge of bird amateurs, knowledge they nevertheless make extensive use of, though without acknowledgement.

4   P. Descola, 'Les Usages de la terre: cosmopolitique de la territorialité' [The uses of land: cosmopolitics of territoriality], lecture (in French) given at the Collège de France, 2 March 2016. On the same subject, see also S. Vanuxem, *La Propriété de la terre*. Marseilles: Wildproject, 2018.

5 For the jurist Grotius (1583–1645), and as Philippe Descola reminds us, individual and collective appropriation was only possible because of the existence of a basic right during the fictional pre-social period, which he refers to as a 'state of nature'. This 'natural' right ensured that each human being had free access to everything: 'Each man could at once take whatever he wished for his own needs, and could consume whatever was capable of being consumed . . . . Whatever each had thus taken for his own use another could not take from him except by an unjust act.'

6 On this subject, see in particular Sarah Vanuxem, who examines the resources of legal history to find ways of modifying the modern conception of ownership. See also, with a view to providing food for thought and envisaging the possibility of a reappropriation of the 'commons', the very fine article written by S. Gutwirth and I. Stengers, 'Le Droit à l'épreuve de la résurgence des commons', *Revue juridique de l'environnement*, 41/2 (2016): 306–43.

7 Cited ibid., p. 312.

8 E. Blaze, 'Mœurs et usages de la vie privée: chasse, vénerie, fauconnerie, oisellerie', in P. Lacroix and F. Seré (eds), *Le Moyen Âge et la Renaissance: histoire et description des mœurs et usages, du commerce et de l'industrie, des sciences, des arts, des littératures et des beaux-arts en Europe*, vol. 1. Paris: Editions Paris Administration, 1848, pp. i–xix. It should be noted that the author points out that, even in the fifteenth century, bird keeping was a profession subject to rules and regulations and bringing with it certain privileges (in particular, that of being able to hang up bird cages in Paris shops without the permission of tenants, and also the right accorded to master bird-catchers to hunt and sell birds).

9 H. E. Howard, *Territory in Bird Life*. London: Collins, [1920] 1948, p. 16.

10 K. Lorenz, *On Aggression*. London: Routledge, 2002, p. 32.

11 I shall deliberately maintain silence, in the text itself, on the subject of Robert Ardrey's book *The Territorial Imperative*, which looks for the instinctive origins of property and nations (no less) within the animal kingdom. Under the pretext of an invitation to humility (let us accept our animal origins and our instincts, and all will be well), the reader finds himself confronted with the return of the most conservative and patriarchal natural law of our social organizations. In order not to waste time, we will simply draw attention to the criticism made by Engels, at the end of the nineteenth century, of social Darwinists, when he denounced what he called 'a conjuring trick': we transpose our concepts, our uses and our categories of society onto nature, then we reapply them to society, and these categories, organizations and uses become natural laws.

12 Nice, 'The role of territory in bird life', p. 470.

13 I. Stengers, *Civiliser la modernité? Whitehead et les ruminations du sens commun*. Dijon: Les Presses du réel, 'Drama' collection, 2017, pp. 135–8.

14 M. Serres, *Malfeasance: Appropriation through Pollution?*. Stanford, CA: Stanford University Press, 2011.

15 M. Serres, *The Natural Contract*. Ann Arbor: University of Michigan Press, 1995, p. 39.

16 M. Serres, *Darwin, Bonaparte et le Samaritain: une philosophie de l'histoire*. Paris: Le Pommier, 2016, p. 16, and onwards for all other quotations in this section.

17 Serres, *Malfeasance*, p. 1.

18 Ibid., p. 3.

19 Ibid., p. 8.

20 Ibid., p. 12.

21 Ibid., p. 3.

22 For the exact reference see ibid., p. 41.

23 J.-C. Bailly, *The Animal Side*. New York: Fordham University Press, 2011.

24 L. Giuggioli, J. R. Potts, D. I. Rubenstein and S. A. Levin, 'Stigmergy, collective actions, and animal social spacing', *Proceedings of the National Academy of Sciences*, 42 (2013): 16904–9.

25 V. Geist, 'On the rutting behavior of the mountain goat', *Journal of Mammology*, 45/4 (1965): 562; H. Hediger, *Wild Animals in Captivity*. London: Butterworths, 1950.

26 R. A. Hinde, 'The biological significance of the territories of birds', *Ibis*, 98 (1956): 340–69, at p. 342.

27 My thanks to Baptiste Morizot, my generous and attentive reader, for drawing my attention to this.

Counterpoint

1 P. Boucheron, 'Ce que peut l'histoire', Inaugural lecture at the Collège de France, Thursday 17 December 2015. For an English version, see 'Of what is History capable?', https://books.openedition.org/cdf/5876?lang=en.

2 Z. Bauman, *Does Ethics Have a Chance in a World of Consumers?*. Cambridge, MA: Harvard University Press, 2009.

3 Ibid., p. 4.

4 Ibid., pp. 5–6.

5 Ibid., p. 5.

6 R. Jones, 'Why insects get such a buzz out of socialising', *The Guardian*, 25 January 2007.

7 S. Sumner, E. Lucas, J. Barker and N. Isaac, 'Radio-tagging technology reveals extreme nest-drifting behavior in a eusocial insect', *Current Biology*, 17/2 (2007): 140–5.

8 Bauman, *Does Ethics Have a Chance?*, p. 9.

9 Note also that the researchers behind this discovery also refer to some previous research, undertaken in 1991, and published in 1998, which

investigated this possibility in wasps (K. J. Pfeiffer and K. Crailsheim, 'Drifting of honeybees', *Insectes Sociaux*, 45/2 (1998): 151–67). While it is true that the most widely favoured hypothesis was that this was the result of social parasitism, this article pointed out that bees are known to move from one nest to another. The authors challenge the idea of parasitism by observing that no attempted thefts were observed and, moreover, note that the bees guarding the hives allowed bees from other hives to enter freely, after inspection, but rejected any individuals suspected of an intention to steal.

10 This information can be found in the very beautiful book by C. Van Acker, *La Bête à bon dos*. Paris: Joseph Corti, 2018, p. 75.

11 Cited by Margaret Morse Nice, 'The role of territory in bird life', *American Midland Naturalist*, 26/3 (1941): 441–87, p. 452.

12 This information can be found in the article about Barbara Blanchard written by S. I. Rothstein, '*In memoriam*: Barbara Blanchard Dewolf, 1912–2008', *The Auk*, 127/1 (2010): 235–7.

Chapter 2 The Power to Affect

1 J. M. Dewar, 'The relation of the oyster-catcher to its natural environment', *Zoologist*, 19 (1915): 281–91, 340–6.

2 The above examples are taken from Margaret Morse Nice, 'The role of territory in bird life', *American Midland Naturalist*, 26/3 (1941): 441–87.

3 R. A. Hinde, 'The biological significance of the territory of birds', *Ibis*, 98 (1956): 340–69.

4 C. Maher and D. Lott, 'A review of the ecological determinants of territoriality within vertebrate species', *American Midland Naturalist*, 143/1 (2000): 1–29.

5 C. Moffat, 'The spring rivalry of birds', *Irish Naturalists' Journal*, 12 (1903): 152–66.

6   É. Souriau, *Le Sens artistique des animaux*. Paris: Hachette, 1965, p. 32.

7   Ibid., p. 102.

8   Ibid., p. 62.

9   The English translation of the citation from Buytendijk was found in J. Moltmann (ed.), *Theology of Play*. New York: Harper & Row, 1972, p. 20.

10 Ferris Jabr quotes the scientist Richard O. Prum in an article dedicated to him, 'How beauty is making scientists rethink evolution', *New York Times*, 9 January 2019.

11 B. Morizot, 'Les animaux intraduisibles', *Billebaude*, no. 14: *Mondes sonores* (2019): 56–66, at p. 61.

12 K. Riebel, M. L. Hall and N. E. Langmore, 'Female songbirds still struggling to be heard', *Trends in Ecology & Evolution*, 8 (2005): 419–20. See also K. Riebel, 'The "mute" sex revisited: vocal production and perception learning in female songbirds', *Advances in the Study of Behavior*, 33 (2003): 49–86.

13 H. E. Howard, *Territory in Bird Life*. London: Collins, [1920] 1948, p. 131.

14 Nice, 'The role of territory in bird life', p. 461.

15 L. L. Wolf and F. G. Stiles, 'Evolution of pair cooperation in a tropical hummingbird', *Evolution*, 24/4 (1970): 759–73. We could compare this hypothesis to what the biologist Richard Dawkins called the extended phenotype, considering for example the bird's nest or the spider's web as extensions of the organism (R. Dawkins, *The Extended Phenotype*. Oxford: Oxford University Press, 1982).

16 J. Verner, 'Evolution of polygamy in the long-billed marsh wren', *Evolution*, 18 (1964): 252–61.

17 W. C. Allee, A. E. Emerson, O. Park, T. Park and K. P. Schmidt, *Principles of Animal Ecology*. Philadelphia: W. B. Saunders, 1949, p. 6.

18 Nice, 'The role of territory in bird life', p. 468.

19 Allee et al., *Principles of Animal Ecology*, p. 8.

20 R. Carrick, 'Ecological significance of territory in the Australian magpie, *Gymnorhina tibicen*', *Proceedings of the 13th International Ornithological Congress* (1963): 740–53.

21 J. Stamps, 'Territorial behavior: testing the assumptions', *Advances in the Study of Behavior*, 23 (1993): 173–232, at p. 176.

Counterpoint

1 B. Latour, *Facing Gaia: Eight Lectures on the New Climatic Regime*. Cambridge: Polity, 2017, p. 271.

2 J. Stamps, 'Territorial behavior: testing the assumptions', *Advances in the Study of Behavior*, 23 (1993): 173–232.

Chapter 3 Overpopulation

1 V. C. Wynne-Edwards, *Evolution through Group Selection*. Oxford: Blackwell Scientific, 1986, p. 6.

2 C. Moffat, 'The spring rivalry of birds', *Irish Naturalists' Journal*, 12 (1903): 152–66, at p. 157.

3 Ibid., p. 153, and onwards for other passages quoted.

4 K. Lorenz, *On Aggression*. London: Routledge, 2002. The book was first published in German in 1963 under the title *Das sogenannte Böse: zur Naturgeschichte der Aggression* (Vienna: Borotha-Schoeler). Note that just one year earlier the British zoologist Vero Copner Wynne-Edwards advanced a very similar hypothesis, which he associated with the theory of group selection. His work received a mixed response. For an analysis of his theory, see my first work: *Naissance d'une théorie éthologique: la danse du cratérope écaillé*. Paris: Les Empêcheurs de penser en rond, 1996 (English edn: *The Dance of the Arabian Babbler: Birth of an Ethological Theory*. Minneapolis: University of Minnesota Press, 2021).

5 Lorenz, *On Aggression*, p. 28.

6 P. A. Kropotkin, *Mutual Aid: A Factor of Evolution*. New York: Dover, 1914.

7 Huyb Kluyver and Lukas Tinbergen, 'Territory and the regulation of diversity in titmice', *Archives Neerlandaises de Zoologie*, 10 (1953): 265–89.

8 W. C. Allee, A. E. Emerson, O. Park, T. Park and K. P. Schmidt, *Principles of Animal Ecology*. Philadelphia: W. B. Saunders, 1949, p. 11.

9 Ibid., p. 399, and following pages.

10 J. Stamps, 'Territorial behavior: testing the assumptions', *Advances in the Study of Behavior*, 23 (1993): 173–232.

Counterpoint

1 F. Raphoz, *Parce que l'oiseau*. Paris: Éditions Corti, 2018, p. 45.

2 Mentioned by D. Lack, 'Early references to territory in bird life', *The Condor*, 46/3 (1944): 108–11, at p. 110.

3 R. E. Stewart and J. W. Aldrich, 'Removal and repopulation of breeding birds in a spruce-fir forest community', *The Auk*, 68/4 (1951): 471–82.

4 J. Mitteldorf, *Aging is a Group Selected Adaptation: Theory, Evidence and Medical Implications*. Boca Raton, FL: CRC Press, 2016.

5 M. Max Hensley and James B. Cope, 'Further data on removal and repopulation of the breeding birds in a spruce-fir forest community', *The Auk*, 68/4 (1951): 483–93.

6 G. H. Orians, 'The ecology of blackbird (*Agelaius*) social systems', *Ecological Monographs*, 31 (1961): 285–312.

7 A. Watson and R. Moss, 'A current model of population dynamics in red grouse', *Proceedings of the 15th International Ornithological Congress* (1972): 134–49.

8 In French, the word 'alliance' has the double meaning of an alliance and

a wedding ring, so ringing the bird has connotations of the commitment of marriage.

9   B. Morizot, 'Ce mal de pays sans exil: les affects du mauvais temps qui vient', *Critiques (Vivre dans un monde abîmé)*, no. 860–861 (2019): 166–81.

10 On this subject, see T. Van Dooren, *Flight Ways: Life and Loss at the Edge of Extinction*. New York: Columbia University Press, 2014.

11 In a fascinating interview conducted by the *Le Monde* journalist Catherine Vincent, Donna Haraway remarks that the Anthropocene could just as easily go under the name of Plantationocene. This term forces us to look closely at the history which preceded industrial capitalism and which was responsible for the conditions of that period: 'What the Plantationocene introduced across the entire world are all the technologies associated with the development and extraction of resources, monoculture, forced displacement of humans and non-humans, including and especially plants, all with the view to constantly maximizing production.' Each of the terms used to describe our era focuses our attention on specific issues and calls for a different engagement. All of them are significant, and it is important to keep on finding other terms which will engage us in different ways. So, for example, Haraway would also suggest our era should be given the name of 'Phonocene', the era of sound, the era where we hear the sounds of the earth, the era which connects us to the power of sound. See the *Idées* supplement to *Le Monde*, 2 February 2019.

Counterpoint

1   G. Deleuze and F. Guattari, *A Thousand Plateaux: Capitalism and Schizophrenia*. London: Continuum, 2003, p. 314.

2   Marcos Matteos Diaz has long been a fellow investigator who has fol-

lowed the progress of each of my research projects with his comments and advice.

3 G. Deleuze, *Abécédaire*, TV documentary, 1986. See English version, *From A to Z*, DVD interview with C. Parnet and G. Deleuze. New York: Semiotexte, 2011.

4 Deleuze and Guattari, *A Thousand Plateaux*, p. 240.

5 D. Haraway, *When Species Meet*. Minneapolis: University of Minnesota Press, 2007.

6 G. Deleuze and C. Parnet, *Dialogues II*. New York: Columbia University Press, 2007, p. 13.

7 I can never thank Isabelle Stengers enough for insisting that I should go back to this book. Her tenacity was all the more commendable given that her reward each time was my bad mood.

8 Reading *Mille Plateaux* seemed, at certain points, so difficult – because I was trying to read them in a controlled way, in other words at an academic level – that I often found myself referring to the English translation. The translator (in this case Brian Massumi), whom I trusted implicitly, had been obliged to make certain choices, choices which indicate a certain type of understanding, which select certain interpretations. In a sense, reading in translation made it seem as if some of my own responsibility was removed.

9 On this subject, see Deleuze and Parnet, *Dialogues II*.

10 Deleuze and Guattari, *A Thousand Plateaux*, p. 11.

11 Ibid., p. 314.

12 Ibid., p. 315.

13 Ibid., p. 317 (or 339).

14 Ibid., p. 324.

15 Deleuze and Parnet, *Dialogues II*, p. 8 (the lyrics in question are: 'Yes I am a thief of thoughts . . . . keys in the wind t'unlock my mind / an' t'grant my closet thoughts backyard air').

Chapter 4 Possessions

1 Margaret Morse Nice, 'The role of territory in bird life', *American Midland Naturalist*, 26/3 (1941): 441–87, at pp. 447–8.

2 H. Hediger, *Wild Animals in Captivity*. London: Butterworths Scientific, 1950, pp. 4–6 for this and subsequent citations.

3 A term which is open to challenge. Indeed, Stéphane Durand informs me on this subject that very few species of birds of prey are cosmopolitan.

4 Translator's note: The French verb 'affecter' means both 'to affect' (or move) and 'to allocate' (or assign).

5 J. Huxley, 'A natural experiment on the territorial instinct', *British Birds*, 27 (1934): 270–7.

6 F. Raphoz, *Parce que l'oiseau*. Paris: Éditions Corti, 2018.

7 This proposal was made following comments made by Thibault De Meyer on reading this section (email of 9 February 2017).

8 D. Lapoujade, *The Lesser Existences: Étienne Souriau, an Aesthetics for the Virtual*. Minneapolis: University of Minnesota Press, 2021, p. 46.

9 S. Vanuxem, *La Propriété de la terre*. Marseilles: Wildproject, 2018, p. 13.

10 G. Deleuze and F. Guattari, *A Thousand Plateaux: Capitalism and Schizophrenia*. London: Continuum, 2003, p. 318.

11 M. de Karangal, *The Heart*. New York: Picador, 2017, pp. 136–7.

Counterpoint

1 T. Rowell, in V. Despret and D. Demorcy, *Non Sheepish Sheep*, documentary produced in the context of the exhibition 'Making Things Public: Atmospheres of Democracy' (directed by B. Latour and P. Weibel), ZKM Karlsruhe, spring 2005.

2 J. Ackerman, *The Genius of Birds: The Intelligent Life of Birds*. London: Corsair, 2016.

3 In Le Guin, *Dancing at the Edge of the World*. New York: Grove Press, 1989.

4 See V. Despret, *Quand le loup habitera avec l'agneau*. Paris: Seuil, 2002.

Chapter 5 Aggression

1 H. E. Howard, *Territory in Bird Life*. London: Collins, [1920] 1948, pp. 79 and 80 for all quotations in this section.

2 Margaret Morse Nice, 'The role of territory in bird life', *American Midland Naturalist*, 26/3 (1941): 441–87, at pp. 468 and 469.

3 J. Stamps and V. Krishnan, 'How territorial animals compete for divisible space: a learning based model', *American Naturalist*, 157 (2001): 154–69.

4 R. C. Ydenberg, L. A. Giraldeau and B. J. Falls, 'Neighbours, strangers and the asymmetric war of attrition', *Animal Behaviour*, 36 (1988): 343–7.

5 Stamps and Krishnan, 'How territorial animals compete for divisible space', p. 165.

6 T. De Meyer, email of 24 January 2019.

7 J.-M. Schaeffer, *Théorie des signaux coûteux, esthétique et art*. Rimouski, Quebec: Tangence éditeur, 2009.

8 J. Fisher, 'Evolution and bird sociality', in J. Huxley, A. C. Hardy and E. B. Ford (eds), *Evolution as a Process*. London: Allen & Unwin, 1954, pp. 71–83.

9 F. Fraser Darling, 'Social behavior and survival', *The Auk*, 69/2 (1952): 183–91.

10 Email of 9 February 2019. Thibault De Meyer's comments are taken from our email exchanges.

Counterpoint

1 G. Schaller, preface to S. Strum, *Almost Human: A Journey into the World of Baboons*. Chicago: University of Chicago Press, 2001.

2 S. Strum and B. Latour, 'Redefining the social link: from baboons to humans', *Social Sciences Information*, 26/4 (1987): 783–802, at p. 788.

3 G. Deleuze, 'Instincts and institutions', in Deleuze, *Desert Islands and Other Texts, 1953–1974*. Cambridge, MA: MIT Press; London: Semiotext(e), 2004, pp. 19–21. I would like to thank my seminar colleagues from the research group Matérialités de la politique at the University of Liège and, in particular, Florence Caeymaex, Édouard Delruelle, Antoine Janvier, Jérôme Flas and Ferhat Taylan who, with enormous generosity, discussed and shared their comments on an early version of my research and gave me some fascinating avenues of research, including this text by Deleuze.

4 Ibid., pp. 20 and 21.

5 S. Strum, 'Darwin's monkey: why baboons can't become humans', *Yearbook of Physical Anthropology*, 55 (2012): 3–23, at p. 14.

6 Ibid., p. 12.

7 Ibid., p. 13.

8 B. Latour, Postscript to S. Strum, *Presque humain: voyage chez les babouins*. St Just la Pendue: Eshel, 1990.

9 On this subject, see D. Haraway, *Primate Visions: Gender, Race, and Nature in the World of Modern Science*. London: Verso, 1992; and S. Strum and L. Fedigan, 'Changing views of primate society: a situated North American view', in Strum and Fedigan (eds), *Primate Encounters: Models of Science, Gender and Society*. Chicago: University of Chicago Press, 2000, pp. 3–49.

Chapter 6 Polyphonic Scores

1 L. Merlini, 'Indices d'architectures', *Revue Malaquais*, no. 1 (2014): 9.

2 J.-Y. Cousteau and F. Dumas, *The Silent World*. New York: Ballantine Books, 1953, p. 170.

3 M. Hansel, *Built by Animals: The Natural History of Animal Architecture*. Oxford: Oxford University Press, 2008, p. 56.

4 E. Souriau, *Le Sens artistique des animaux*. Paris: Hachette, 1965, p. 88.

5 First of all because, in a previous research project on altruism in birds, dunnocks clearly stood out from all other birds for their highly inventive and remarkably adaptive behaviour (with the exception of one other species – the Arabian babbler, which I eventually decided to focus on for my research; see *The Dance of the Arabian Babbler: Birth of an Ethological Theory*. Minneapolis: University of Minnesota Press, 2021). Also because, in my home town, Albert Demaret, brilliant bird observer that he was, once told me that, each New Year's Day, a dunnock would come and sing on top of the same block of flats with absolutely astonishing punctuality – flexibility and reliability – this is the hallmark of habit.

6 N. B. Davies and A. Lundberg, 'Food distribution and a variable mating system in the Dunnock, *Prunella modularis*', *Journal of Animal Ecology*, 53/3 (1984): 895–912.

7 W. C. Allee, A. E. Emerson, O. Park, T. Park and K. P. Schmidt, *Principles of Animal Ecology*. Philadelphia: W. B. Saunders, 1949, p. 393.

8 J. Stamps, 'Conspecific attraction and aggregation in territorial species', *American Naturalist*, 11/3 (1988): 329–47.

9 Margaret Morse Nice, 'The role of territory in bird life', *American Midland Naturalist*, 26/3 (1941): 441–87, at p. 463.

10 Ibid., p. 456.

11 Allee et al., *Principles of Animal Ecology*, p. 417.

12 J. Stamps, 'Territorial behavior: testing the assumptions', *Advances in the Study of Behavior*, 23 (1993): 173–232, at p. 220.

13 Ibid.

14 B. Krause, *The Great Animal Orchestra: Finding the Origins of Music in the World's Wild Places*. London: Profile Books, 2013, p. 99.

15 Ibid., p. 98.

16 Ibid., pp. 87–8.

17 B. B. DeWolfe, L. F. Baptista and Lewis Petrinovich, 'Song development and territory establishment in Nuttall's white-crowned sparrows', *The Condor*, 91/2 (1989): 397–407.

18 Michel Kreutzer refers to research on song matching by Jean-Claude Brémond. M. Kreutzer, *L'Éthologie*. Paris: Que sais-je?, 2017, p. 104.

19 Translator's note: The word 'partition' in France means both a musical store and the partition or division of an area or country into separate parts or sections.

20 B. Morizot, *Les Diplomates: cohabiter avec les loups sur une autre carte du vivant*. Marseilles: Wildproject, 2016, p. 71.

21 J. Fisher, 'Evolution and bird sociality', in J. Huxley, A. C. Hardy and E. B. Ford (eds), *Evolution as a Process*. London: Allen & Unwin, 1954, pp. 71–83.

22 R. C. Ydenberg, L. A. Giraldeau and B. J. Falls, 'Neighbours, strangers and the asymmetric war of attrition', *Animal Behaviour*, 36 (1988): 343–7.

23 É. Briefer, F. Rybak and T. Aubin, 'When to be a dear enemy: flexible acoustic relationships of neighbouring skylarks, *Alauda arvensis*', *Animal Behaviour*, 76 (2008): 1319–25, at p. 1324.

24 See, for example, in the context of south-east Peru, C. A. Munn and J. W. Terborgh, 'Multi-species territoriality in neotropical foraging flocks', *The Condor*, 81/4 (1979): 338–47; or, with reference to colonies in French Guyana, M. Jullien and J.-M. Thiollay, 'Multi-species ter-

ritoriality and dynamic of neotropical forest understorey bird flocks', *Journal of Animal Ecology*, 67 (1998): 227–52.

25 J. H. Crook, 'The adaptive significance of avian social organisations', *Symposia of the Zoological Society of London*, no. 14 (1965): 181–218.

26 B. Heinrich, *Winter World: The Ingenuity of Animal Survival*. New York: HarperCollins, 2004, p. 246.

27 Translator's note: The French expression for public transport is 'les transports en commun', meaning 'shared' transport.

28 R. Malavasi and A. Farina, 'Neighbours' talk: interspecific choruses among songbirds', *Bioacoustics*, 22/1 (2013): 1–16.

29 The French phrase 'le courage chanté des oiseaux' is a reference to the title of a song by Dominique A, 'Le courage des oiseaux', from the album *Un disque sourd* (1991).

Counterpoint

1 C. Lamarche, *Nous sommes à la lisière*. Paris: Gallimard, 2019, p. 153.

Gathering up the Knowledge which has Fallen from the Nest

1 This investigative space is described in J.-C. Passeron, *Sociological Reasoning: A Non-Popperian Space of Argumentation*. Oxford: Bardwell Press, 2013.